Walking Backwards
to Christmas

Walking Backwards to Christmas

STEPHEN COTTRELL

WJK WESTMINSTER
JOHN KNOX PRESS
LOUISVILLE · KENTUCKY

First published in Great Britain in 2014
by the Society for Promoting Christian Knowledge

Published in the United States of America in 2015 by
Westminster John Knox Press
100 Witherspoon Street
Louisville, KY 40202

15 16 17 18 19 20 21 22 23 24—10 9 8 7 6 5 4 3 2 1

Scripture quotations are taken or adapted from the New Revised Standard Version of the Bible, Anglicized Edition, copyright © 1989, 1995 by the Division of Christian Education of the National Council of the Churches of Christ in the USA. Used by permission. All rights reserved.

Cover design by designpointinc.com
Cover art: Nativity with Burning Bush, Herbert, Albert (1925–2008), courtesy of Private Collection, England and Co. Gallery, London/Bridgeman Images

Library of Congress Cataloging-in-Publication Data

Cottrell, Stephen.
 Walking backwards to Christmas / Stephen Cottrell.
   pages cm
 Originally published: London : Society for Promoting Christian Knowledge, 2014.
 ISBN 978-0-664-26186-3 (alk. paper)
 1. Christmas. I. Title.
 BV45$b .C677 2015
 242'.335--dc23

                                                        2015013016

♾The paper used in this publication meets the minimum requirements of the American National Standard for Information Sciences—Permanence of Paper for Printed Library Materials, ANSI Z39.48-1992.

For all those who thought they knew the story well

In him was life,
and the life was the light of all people.
The light shines in the darkness,
and the darkness did not overcome it.

(John 1.4–5)

Contents

Acknowledgments

I am grateful to Joanna Moriarty and Alison Barr at SPCK and other colleagues here in Chelmsford for their encouragement with this book.

Richard Harries introduced me to the paintings of Albert Herbert. You can find out more in his book *The Image of Christ in Modern Art*.

When it came to imagining how Mary might respond to the created world around her I chanced upon the Palestine-Family.net website and Lucy Nusseibeh's wonderfully informative essay, 'Palestinian Flowers: Indigenous Symbols of Strength and Hope'. The Holy Land Restorers website was also helpful with information about trees in Palestine.

The chapter from the perspective of Isaiah draws massively on the biblical text, but I have only used speech marks to denote this on a few occasions. It just seemed better to weave the biblical narrative into what I have written and imagined in as seamless a way as possible. But I did think this needed acknowledging. I hope biblical purists will forgive me.

I also feel obliged to point out that I am aware that Isaiah is best understood as three books, not one, and in drawing material from the biblical text I have taken passages from all three. But each element that now comes to us as the one book of the prophet has vital things to say about who the Messiah will be. Consequently, it seemed legitimate, in a book like this, to use this material, spoken as it were from darkness, to point towards the light.

Introduction

Sometimes people ask me how I find time to write. The only sensible answer I can come up with is that we all find time for the things that really give us joy.

It has been a joy to write this book. Encouraged by the success of *The Nail*, which retold the Good Friday story through the voices of different characters involved in the drama of that day, this book retells the Christmas story. But because this story is so well known—possibly the only bit of the Christian story that is still familiar to most people— I have used the device of telling the story backwards. The idea for this came to me in a flash when I first saw Albert Herbert's painting *Nativity with Burning Bush*, which is reproduced on the front cover of this book. From left to right we see Joseph (or is it one of the shepherds?); then the infant Jesus being held up for him to see; then Mary herself; and then the bright, vivid image of the burning bush. It is a strange and evocative painting. There is (for me, at any rate) a movement across the canvas that appears to be going backwards from the person who beholds the presence of Christ, to Christ himself, and then to Mary, who so obviously has a central place in the story, and then behind Mary to the burning bush.

In the traditional iconography of the Orthodox Church it is not unusual for the burning bush, through which Moses heard the voice of God, to be a sign of the Virgin Mary. This is not something we are used to in Western art. But with deceptively brilliant simplicity, Herbert's primitive and deliberately childlike depictions of the biblical narrative draw together our contemporary adoration of Christ, with the nativity itself, and with God's revelation of himself and his name to Moses—that name, and that word which is made flesh in Christ. The painting does what all good paintings do. A complex web of ideas— and in this case a complex narrative—is captured in a single image. I hope my book does what good books can do, which is get underneath the skin of a story and begin to tell it in such a way as we can see ourselves in it, aiming to uncover the complex web of motive and response. I had been thinking for some time of writing a book about the Christmas story; the apparent backwards movement in this painting, and the way the painting dramatically introduces the revelation to Moses in the burning bush alongside the birth of Christ, suggested a backwards way of telling the story. From this moment the book was born. And once I remembered that Christmas hit by the Goons I had a title for the book as well. Writing it was a joyful thing.

The Nail has been used by many parishes, not just as a book to read and study in Lent, but also liturgically as a series of

Introduction

Good Friday meditations. When I started writing this book
I had similar ideas about how it might be used at Christmas,
even as a sort of adult nativity play, with people taking different parts and retelling the story from their perspective. I
suppose this could still be done, but what I have found excit-
ing about writing this book is the way the retelling of the
story from the perspective of different people in it has led me
to encounter quite directly the many uncertainties and horrors in what turns out to be quite a dark story. These bits—
the intrigues of Herod, the massacre of the innocents, the
uncertainties of Joseph and Zechariah—are not usually told.
I have been reminded that although the Christmas story is
well known, most of us have learned it from school nativity plays and carols. On the whole this version of the story
is more concerned with light than darkness. The backwards
approach I have taken here allows the movement to be in the
opposite direction. Hence I decided to start with the pres-
entation of Christ in the Temple as the Light of the World
(and by the way, this is another scene that Albert Herbert
has depicted in his paintings) and end with the prophecies
of Isaiah and the revelation to Moses. I was also struck by
the central place that women have in the drama, and I have
enjoyed trying to inhabit their experience and find their
voice. This is why I have chosen to start with Anna, rather
than Simeon. And so that I could uncover the whole narrative I found it useful to hear the voice of another witness
to the birth itself; since there was no one in the Scriptures I
could turn to, I have used the innkeeper's wife, a character

who appears nowhere in Matthew's or Luke's birth narratives, but is a popular fixture in nativity plays. I hope this poetic license, along with a great many others, will be forgiven. But in every other aspect of the book, it has been meditating on the biblical story that has been my chief inspiration. I simply want to tell the story—in its light and in its darkness—in a way that will enable people to encounter it as if for the first time. Consequently, it is not your usual Christmas book. But I hope it is one that will stimulate and inspire.

As I was writing I found aspects of myself in the different characters. I think you will find the same. I hope that you may be encouraged to put on some sort of adult nativity play, based around the idea of first-person narratives retelling the story, although the chapters here are probably a bit long to be used.

I think it is best to read the book alone, like a novel. But if you know of other people doing the same, then why not spend an evening, perhaps just before Christmas, responding together to what you have read—and, hopefully, to the new vistas in the story that this book has opened up. Just asking these few questions should be enough for a useful and enjoyable evening's discussion. It might even help you start some sort of book club in your church community or neighborhood.

- Which person in the story did you most relate to?
- What surprised, shocked or delighted you the most?
- How has this changed your understanding of the Christmas story?

Chapter 1

———◆———

Anna

There was also a prophet, Anna the daughter of Phanuel, of the tribe of Asher. She was of a great age, having lived with her husband for seven years after her marriage, then as a widow to the age of eighty-four. She never left the temple but worshipped there with fasting and prayer night and day. At that moment she came, and began to praise God and to speak about the child to all who were looking for the redemption of Jerusalem.

Luke 2.36–38

Anna

Light.

I have always longed for its warmth and brightness: enjoyed the high noon of its Mediterranean intensity; seen its power to illuminate and burn. And I have wanted it inside me; there is an accumulation of darkness and regret that only the direct attention of something brighter than the sun can cleanse and penetrate, and burn away the flotsam of a lifetime.

That is why I came to the Temple, why I made it my home, why I put up with the taunts of those who thought me mad; though I suppose my daily date with the rising sun, and my dogged insistence that a greater light was coming, is a kind of madness. Most people are able to settle for less, and make amends with mediocrity. Not me. I longed for something more, for a fire that burns brightly without consuming.

My husband died after we had been married only seven years. In his death I felt cheated of the life I had expected. Weeks blurred into years as I imagined him back, or around the corner somewhere close, or thought bereavement could be healed. I bore the aching loneliness of grief like one who strikes a spade against dry ground and never makes even the smallest impression, and I was exhausted; or like one who searches every corner of every room, day after day, over and over, searching and searching, but never finding what is lost, never even really knowing what to look for: knowing it is gone, but never calling off the search. Futile, empty and broken, I poured out my days like cold water onto hot metal; and my life was dispersed on the air. Forgotten.

Sometimes I would wake in the night and imagine him back with me. It was even as if I could feel his arms around me and his hands upon me, his fingers searching out my flesh and his warm mouth upon my neck. And I would be exultant, charged. But the moment of waking was also the moment of knowledge, grim and sober, and I was alone. When you are alone, and when you are empty, memories are little comfort. They sting like salt on freshly opened wounds. But I cannot forget either.

But I am Anna, daughter of Phanuel, and a prophet. I know pain and isolation. I know longing. And slowly my longing changed. Not for him that was lost—though I long for him still—but for him who is the source of longing and desire; who fashioned love; who added sinew to limb, and molded flesh on bone, and poured a lifeblood in our veins; who breathed his spirit in us, and raised us out of dust; who gave us to each other, and showed us love. And though for me love has been too fleeting and too hard, I will not deride it, nor make room for scorn. I have discovered a different searching and a different longing.

And my path led to Jerusalem. To the Temple. This is where I dwell, where I have been dwelling many years. I am now an old woman—eighty-four years young—and I live in the

Temple at Jerusalem. Here in its darkness, in its comforting shadow: which I believe is the shadow of something greater than all the greatness of the world. This is the place where, one day, a greater light will dawn.

That has been the focus of my longing: a new light. Each new dawn is for me a presage of that light. I do the same each day. I find the exact place in the Temple where the first rays of the rising sun will suddenly flood its dark interior, and wait there. For when the sun has made its steady progress round the globe I know there will be a particular moment when a single beam of bright morning sunlight shafts from a high solitary window in the east wall and crafts a narrow illuminating passage of light down the center of the Temple's spaciousness. I love that moment. I wait for it each day. I plan for it. I am meticulous. I have studied the pattern of the galaxies and seen how the movement of the stars conspires to create such astonishing newness each day. And having drawn my conclusions I stand in the spot each day where I know the sun will catch me, flood me, fill me. And as it rises and its beams grow stronger, they travel the length of the Temple, and search out everything. And sometimes I stand right at the back of the Temple and watch the light moving inexorably towards me, and wait in glorious expectation for it to strike. I stretch out my hands; and though I know you cannot hold sunlight, you can feel it upon you. I close my eyes and wait simply to touch its presence—which isn't me touching at all, but being touched, held in warmth and light. I bathe in its luminescent brightness. And if I opened my eyes and looked up, why, I could be blinded. For I know that the very brightest light comes to us as dazzling darkness.

In this light each day I have waited for another light, and learned to love it more. I have dwelt in the pitch darkness of the Temple's night and dreamed of unimaginably beautiful light. In my mind I have danced in its embrace, felt the spectrum of its color upon me, and my inner thoughts are read at last, and understood. There have been nights when I could almost feel the building itself crying out for something greater, for the something it had been made for. Over the years, I have become someone who watches and prays. Such people, I know, are irritating, especially around the religious professionals who ply their trade within these walls and too easily forget what they were built to cherish and uphold. Or else, far worse, imagine such things can be contained and controlled in buildings made by human hands.

When the greater light dawns, this will be swept away. I came to know this. Saw it in the darkness as much as in the light. Dreamed it, and felt it in the nightly shift from deep dark to bright dawning sunlight. I kept a lonely vigil on behalf of a people who had forgotten what they were waiting for; who read their Scriptures and really thought that they pointed here. I came here not because I think that is right, but because this place is an arrow pointing somewhere else, and I believed that I was more likely to see where that somewhere else might be if I looked long enough *from* here, rather than *to* here. I seem like a fixture—that weird old woman who haunts the Temple. But I am the only one who is actually bent on leaving. I came here to find a way out, not a way in. I want the business of this place to be finished. I need a light to show me the way. I glimpse it momentarily in the first bright beams of the dawn; but I wait for it through the long, slow hours of the day. I dream it in the shadows of the night. The light of the world is not Jerusalem, as far as I can tell.

But there is one other. And of course he was in the Temple today as well. Old Simeon. He sees it as I do, though we rarely exchange many words. But I know enough to know that he knows.

Like me, he has been waiting a lifetime. Like me, he waits for that light which is beyond the light of morning: a light that the light of morning depends on and bows before; a light that is brighter and deeper than the noonday sun at its height. And he believes, like me, that the light is coming, and that his life will not be over until that light comes here to the Temple to take over its work of shining brightly.

It is a comfort to know this. For Simeon is a good man. Devout. And in this respect he is not like me. Not full of wildness and dreaming.

God's spirit seems to rest on him. He exudes an affable peacefulness. People turn to him. And he is happy to listen. There is a balm in his presence. And he has been told that he will not see death before he has seen God's blessed one, what we Jews call Messiah. That was why he came to the Temple today. He kind of knew that today was different—that it was a beginning. I didn't know that, not when I stood in the Temple this morning, like I do each day, finding the place where the light can get me. But he seemed to know. When I saw him entering the Temple, I sensed something in him that was different. He was looking around him with an additional eagerness. Old men do not have a spring in their step. The grind of time has already put paid to that. But there was an optimistic sparkle in his eye that seemed for a moment as bright as the sun that had enveloped me in the morning's first rush of light. It was as if he was shimmering with the reflected light of something wonderful.

Then it happened. A moment that changes history, but is of itself undramatic and unnoticed. No clouds parted and no great lights shone. There was no clear separation of light and darkness, like I see each morning, only two people—an older man and a tired younger woman—tramping into the courts of the Temple, looking about them anxiously to find where to go and what to do, and carrying with them something very precious.

Everyone else gets on with their business. There is lots to do, and other parents and other children, and nothing obvious to mark these two out as special. In a way, that is the beauty of it. I see that now in the evening of this, the first day. The light has come into the world, but the world does not know it. And the light has dimmed itself, or should I say clothed itself, in the gray ambiguity of life.

The couple have come for purification, as the Law of Moses prescribes; every firstborn male must be designated as holy to the Lord. They must offer the sacrifice that is stated in the law: that is, a pair of turtle doves or two young pigeons. There is nothing unusual about this. I see it every day. But today, for some reason I have yet managed to fathom, it appalled me. It seemed so necessary and yet so useless. It is the business of the Temple to spill blood, to offer sacrifices to God, to do what the law requires, and then God will be with us. And there is a sacrifice each year that is greater than the rest, when the high priest takes the blood of the Passover Lamb and enters the Holy of Holies and we are all purified. But now I'm asking why? And now I'm asking how? Why this endless death and spilling of blood? What sort of a God needs this slaughter? How does it make a difference, and is there a way of doing what the Temple does that could bring it once and for all to an end?

So the couple do what they have come to do. Even then I didn't know who they were.

That was when Simeon arrived. His eyes darting this way and that, searching the faces in the crowd. When he sees them, even though everyone else carries on just the same, I notice a gladsome stillness in him. I see what he sees: this couple, the tiny little child they carry. The light of the world come among us.

Simeon rushes up to them, sweeps them up in the evident security of his goodness and delight. There is no demurring. He takes the child in his arms. There is only consolation. Consolation for Simeon that his wait is over; but also consolation for the parents, whose own agony of waiting and wondering I can hardly begin to imagine. At last someone else sees and knows what is happening. In his joy and exultation Simeon confirms the hard-won convictions of their journey. They all smile at each other—that kind of silly grinning that is the fruit of recognition and doesn't need words.

But when Simeon does speak, scales fall. He praises God, saying that at last he can depart in peace and, in time, leave the world behind him, for he has seen with his own eyes the salvation of God and the fulfilment of God's promises, not just to Israel, but to the whole world.

That is the truly remarkable thing about what happened today: this child is not just the light of Israel, but the light of the world; a light that burns more brightly than the sun, but a light that is come among us in such a way that we won't be burned; a light that kindles the fire in human hearts; a light that warms and consoles, illuminates and cheers.

The parents are amazed. What he says seems to go beyond even their own fearful expectations. And sensing their confusion, Simeon blesses them. At the same time he says to the mother (I didn't know her name): 'This child is destined for the falling and the rising of many in Israel, and to be a sign that will be opposed so that the inner thoughts of many will be revealed—and a sword will pierce your own soul too.'

It is these words I sit with this evening, watching the daylight fade.

It is the hour for lamps to be lit. But the light I've received today defeats all darkness and I am happy to let what is left of it surround me. It carries no fear. But these words that Simeon spoke, they caused me to cry out with anguish and joy in the Temple this morning. For this light, which we can't yet see as light, this little child that shows us God, will shine within us and reveal everything. And the path ahead will not be easy, for it is to this child that the Temple and all its ceremonies and covenants point to. And if there is any more blood to be spilled, then it will probably be his: this little boy who is God's light for the world. How could a mother not share such pain? As I looked into her face I could see it was already begun, for every mother shares the joy and anguish of every son. Why would this mother—dare I use these words?—the mother of the Lord be any different? No, surely such joy and such pain will be multiplied for such a mother holding such a son?

So there I stood, looking for all to see like a mad woman possessed, but actually feeling more like a young woman released. I thanked God for the strange beauty of his coming among us, and the inscrutable mystery of his ways, that we could see him face-to-face, the dazzling light of his glory, and not be blinded or undone. I jabbered away. My relief. My praise. My amazement at God's provision.

A light has come among us. It has come suddenly, like the dawning of a new day. It has been prepared for from the beginning of time. The light and darkness that were separated at the beginning of creation are united again, and one has overcome the other.

People think me crazier than ever, sitting here in the gathering gloom, shouting out my praises to God, inhabiting the Temple but looking beyond it. But if they had occupied that moment today like I saw it and felt it, then they too would know the satisfaction of waiting and the faithfulness of God.

But no one else did see. That is the infuriating mystery of it. Why do some see, and not others? And where is that tiny scrap of life I saw today really leading?

But I know this, and I know it more than ever: all the busyness of the Temple and the busyness of the world cannot turn back the pages of what has happened today. All we can do is see where it came from and see where it leads us. And if others are to find this light then it will not necessarily be by looking, so much as by waiting and wanting. I have had to allow myself to be found, and this has changed me. My hurts and regrets are still there. But now they are known and illuminated, integrated and healed. And this will be true for others. They too will be enabled to make the offering of themselves and be irradiated. Only then will all our alms and oblations have meaning.

Now it is night again, and I am waiting for the dawn of tomorrow. But it will not be the same. The sun will rise, but it will rise on a different world, a world into which a greater light has come. And in the revelation of tomorrow's dawn I will be embraced by God. It will burst upon me, but this time it will not be a portent of the future but confirmation of today's radiance. I will be gripped by the brightness of the morning sun and my years will slip away.

Chapter 2

Rachel

When Herod saw that he had been tricked by the wise men, he was infuriated, and he sent and killed all the children in and around Bethlehem who were two years old or under, according to the time that he had learned from the wise men. Then was fulfilled what had been spoken through the prophet Jeremiah: 'A voice was heard in Ramah, wailing and loud lamentation, Rachel weeping for her children; she refused to be consoled, because they are no more.'

Matthew 2.16–18

Rachel

I can't scream anymore. Except for a lifetime. So I will keep on shouting out.

There isn't any sound. It is pitched far too high, and it echoes around the empty cavern that was my heart.

My throat is too raw for screaming, but I keep on screaming. I will let my cries go on unceasing, till they come and tear my tongue from my mouth. And then I will probably laugh, and let the dogs lick it up. Because I don't care. I don't give a shit about what is decorous or right. I am all pain. All horror. I am red hot chili thrust into your eyeball. I am hot coal in your loins. I am everything you fear, your darkest nightmare.

You know that terrible, hurting numbness when you hit your thumb with a hammer, or trap your finger in a door. That is me. Everywhere. Always. My eyes emptied of tears, dry like a desert, parched like the river you walk to in the hottest hour of the day and find empty. And my heart also, drained of hope, just a twitching corpse hung up in the chamber of my flesh. My brain shaken like a maraca, banged and pounded like a drum. Even the hairs on my head are aching with grief. There is a burning anger in my bones that makes me want to tear my own flesh to pieces. I am blind rage. I am deaf futility. I am dumb, numb pain. I am horror.

Rachel

And now you want me to explain. But I cannot explain, there is no explaining. I will tell you my story, but I will tell it with howls of grief, and I will not be consoled. I don't want the hope you think you can offer, because it is not hope at all. I am on fire, and you cannot put me out.

Or shall I tell it like a witness statement? Bland and matter of fact. I was there. I saw what happened. It was ghastly. Unspeakably so. This was the time. That was the place. These were the persons involved. This was the outcome. I see the images in my head. I turn the horror over. But it didn't happen to me. It is someone else's nightmare. I just saw it, and now I'm telling you what I saw.

But it was me. And even though I keep on thinking that it is possible to go back to those moments before it happened and change the future, I cannot go back, except to that single moment of terrifying intrusion. So I will tell you in the staccato rhythm of repeated hammer blows on your skull, or like a body flung from a cliff and bouncing on the rocks, or like your fingernails being pulled out one at a time.

They came. Out of nowhere. Swift feet upon the pavement in that early hour when the light begins to come and there is a smudge of vermilion on the eastern sky.

There was no warning. The order had been given and, no sooner given, carried out.

Fists beating on the door. Terrified foreboding in the air. 'Who is it?' 'What is the matter?' and 'Why are you calling at this ungodly hour?'

I remember my voice as they hammered on the door, and it feels like it belonged to someone else. Another woman in another lifetime.

More pounding. Insistent. Unrelenting. My mouth dry. The door pulled an inch ajar and then thrust open. Hands pushing me aside. Eyes darting this way and that. Staring and searching with cold calculation. Three stolid men towering over me. Sweat pearling their brows. The smell of cloves and tannin on their breath. Faces close to mine. One of them has a glob of sticky spittle at the corner of his mouth. Another a single, large stubby hair on his nose. Hands grip my shoulders. Shaking. Demanding. And then, words of dread: 'Madam, don't delay us any longer. We have our orders. Where is the boy?'

Then, in a horrid moment of recollection, swimming in my fuddled brain, my mind filled with the noises of the night, the whimpering and helpless crying of other mothers and of other sons.

And how do you hide a baby boy in a noisy house in the first light of a new day? Even as I trembled in their presence, too terrified to breathe a word, wanting to throw myself across my child or tell them they were mistaken, there was no boy here . . . he is calling me, gurgling and fluttering to life in the makeshift cot at the end of my bed, smiling at the fingers of light that have inched their way into the room through the netting by the window, speckling the room with a hazy brightness and catching in singular definition the motes of dust that are thrown up in the room.

They turn. They push me away. I scream. One long, terrible cry that comes from the center of my bowels and can never be silenced. I jump up to stop them, and one of them holds me down. Holds me and grips my throat like it is nothing, just a pod he could snap open.

It happens. In terrible slow motion. One of them moves to the cot. He picks up my little child, my firstborn son, my joy. At first he is holding him fondly, for who cannot be brought to silly wonder by the gentle eagerness of a baby. And only ten months old. Not yet learned to walk or speak or fear. The world is to be trusted, and here in your mother's house, in your mother's presence, is all safety.

And I remember holding him. Remember it now in this evening's terrible emptiness. I stare into the night and cradle the hollow desperation of the day, rock back and forth humming the lullabies that soothed him to sleep and are all I have left for comfort. And it is no comfort at all.

I remember his birth. The exultant cries of life sliding into the world when the cord was broken and he was delivered out of the floodwaters of my womb and onto my breast and into my arms. I held his little face next to mine. I smothered him with kisses and told him he was dearly loved and wanted more than he could ever know. Each day I held him, and whispered stories of tenderness and beauty into his tiny ears. I wanted him to overflow. I wanted him to know the joys of loving and of being loved. For there is no life, except we know security and affirmation; and too many of the world's wrongs stem from never knowing you are loved. I wanted him brimmed over. I wanted, for him, no doubt that he mattered, that the world was his.

And he grew. Suckled at my breast, he received everything he needed. My warmth and my love and my nurturing made him. My body fed and provided for his body. And though the cord was broken we were still one, held in a grip that only sons and mothers know. His eyes would sparkle when I came into the room. His little hands would reach for me. His pleasure was complete in me.

Then, in that dreadful turned over and turned over moment— just this morning and already an eternity away, the echo of another lifetime in another land—his little fingers curl around the rough flesh of the man's big hands. I wonder how it feels to do what this man did. Do you put it to the back of your mind? Another day's work done. Brutal, but necessary.

Or does it pick away at your soul, hollowing out your heart from the inside, till you are just a shell of a man, an empty vessel; what seems like a man, but only a walking ghost; the outer remains of a man, when inside there is only emptiness and hurt.

Now he is giving that same emptiness to me, taking what is vital, what matters most.

We will share this terrible emptiness: he through the callous cruelty of his work, me through the rage and disappointment that is rooted in my soul and is already eating it away.

What hope is there for us? How can any of us be forgiven? Me, the sinned against, and he, the sinner? Does he do his work so well because his heart is also numb? Is he the product of pain? Will I become like him? Is this where suffering ends, giving it out to others?

There is ominous silence. Outside, two crows begin to caw at each other across the street. A dog starts barking. There are other fearful sounds of crying beginning to fill the air. It is all horribly predictable. Unstoppable. I am overpowered. The forces of something beyond me are upon me.

For there is another child. And I have heard of this other child. He is danger and threat. He is danger and threat to my child. The rumors and the gossip even reached our little village. A new king born in Bethlehem, just as the prophets had said. And Herod's pride erupted. His anger kindled. And when he cries little children die in the streets. There would be no rival to his throne. And it didn't matter if a thousand little boys perished, if this little life could be extinguished. And now. Now, here and now in my house, my security invaded, every little light must be snuffed out to serve the bigger vanity of a weak king. And who cares if God has visited his people, and, if the prophet's words are true, we can even stop God: after all, how many regiments does God have? A pogrom across the land, which I had heard of but not believed. I thought that it would spend its energy before it reached me—like a tempest turned to a breeze. I thought that our little world was safe. A terrible devastation has visited me. I am overpowered. I am helpless to stop it.

He, the man who held my child, held my future. He turned and looked at me. And I looked at him.

And I wanted to say to him, 'You don't have to do this', because I could see that's what he was thinking. But no words came out.

The outside world was very noisy then. I knew what it was, the screaming, the barking, the retching. It was other mothers mourning other sons in the awful massacre of a bright new dawn. How could I have been so blind to the horror? I will blame myself forever.

Rachel

But there was a silence between us in that moment. We both knew what the other was thinking and what the other would do.

My eyes pleaded with him. There was no other way to speak. He saw my begging, my utter helplessness in that moment. I was held down. I was squeezed out. Even the screaming stopped for a moment. And he just said again, 'We have our orders.' Then he pulled a slim, steel blade from beneath his tunic and quickly, like you might slice a fig on a summer's day, slit my son's throat.

Oh, the warm flow of his blood. His brief life briefly shed. The milky film of tears across his closing eyes. A sigh. And gone. Extinguished.

I shuddered then and choked. Gasping for air, I knew there would never be any hope for me. I stare, silently raging against the gathering blackness of the night. My light has gone out.

I don't hate this other child. Jesus, they say his name is. I desire him no ill. But I can't help wishing he hadn't been born. His birth has brought death to me, has brought my little life into the center of things and snuffed out the brief life of my little son; and though I cannot see what good it would do if he was killed as well, I know they are after him, chasing him down. I know his mother's fear, as I know the fear of so many other mothers hiding their children away. In the end they will get him. These earthly powers are not quenched. They have their way. They persist. His blood will be spilled as well. And what good will that do?

Chapter 3

Herod

When King Herod heard this, he was frightened, and all Jerusalem with him; and calling together all the chief priests and scribes of the people, he inquired of them where the Messiah was to be born. They told him, 'In Bethlehem of Judea; for so it has been written by the prophet: "And you, Bethlehem, in the land of Judah, are by no means least among the rulers of Judah; for from you shall come a ruler who is to shepherd my people Israel." Then Herod secretly called for the wise men and learned from them the exact time when the star had appeared. Then he sent them to Bethlehem, saying, 'Go and search diligently for the child; and when you have found him, bring me word so that I may also go and pay him homage.'

Matthew 2.3–8

The exercise of power is lonely and precise. It cannot be shared, and it cannot be ducked. Would you lead an army in two directions at once? Of course not. But someone has to decide. So about the matter of Jesus, born 'king of the Jews', excuse my irritation, I will be brief, but clear. For I am one who knows human folly like the back of my hand.

I first heard of him some weeks ago. Three travelers arrived from the east. Soothsayers and seers they seemed to be, wise men, the sort who study scrolls, and read the skies, and understand the movement of the planets. They were a strange crew, worn out from their traveling, but also zealous and intense. They had seen a new star rising and believed it was a sign that a new king was born. So naturally, they came here, to Jerusalem, to the palace: this is where kings are born.

But I never liked them, and if you want the truth, I never trusted them either. There was something bewitching and fanatical about their pursuit of this king. For are there not many palaces across the nations of the world, and many princes born? Why travel so far for this one? What did it mean? And I don't mind telling you, though it seems laughable now, I was frightened of them, or at least frightened of what they were supposing, for they had indeed traveled all this way on the whim and the whisper of a new star, and they were looking for a child, a king to whom they could give their homage. And there was no king here, except for me.

But I thought I could beguile them. I thought I could win them over. So I called together my own chief priests and scribes, and asked them about our own prophecies, for if this king they spoke of was not born here, then was this some other augury about a king who was himself—and this is the fearful thing—a ruler of kings, a messiah? So I inquired of them, 'Where is the promised Messiah to be born?' And they replied, 'In Bethlehem of Judea; for so it has been written by the prophet: "And you, Bethlehem, in the land of Judah, are by no means least among the rulers of Judah; for from you shall come a ruler who is to shepherd my people Israel."'

So, quietly and secretly, I called those wise men back again. I tolerated them. I welcomed them as if they were kings themselves. I fed them. I looked after their animals. I flattered them, for who is there who does not want to be admired? I told them how wise they were, and how brave. I told them what they wanted to hear. My slave girls bathed them and pampered them and dressed them and were at their disposal. They too are from the east, and know how to please a weary traveler. And they were putty in my hands. They drank my wine, they purred at my compliments, and when replete I questioned them again about this king and about this star and what portent it might have. And their tongues wagged, for who is there who is not susceptible to food and wine . . . and other things? And who doesn't love to talk about himself?

So they told me their interminable stories: the things they had seen, the hardships they had endured. They told me of their tenacity and their resolve. They told me of the companionship they had found on the road, the hospitality they had received (though none better than mine, I imagine!) and the dangers they had faced.

But their words made no sense; and as they talked I realized they really didn't know anything other than their own starstruck madness. So all I discovered was exactly when the star had risen, and the details of the journey they had made. It was then that I also realized that what they needed was my knowledge, and if I gave it they could become my envoys. So I told them about our prophecies and about the ancient dreams of the people I ruled. I sent them to Bethlehem, saying, 'Go and search diligently for the child; and when you have found him, bring me word so that I may also go and pay him homage.'

In the morning they left. I bade them farewell. I pointed them in the right direction. Guiding star, indeed! I smiled at them. I thanked them for their company. I gave them food and spices, wine and blankets and fine linen, and they loaded it onto their donkeys. They thanked me, assuring me that they would return after they had found the infant king. They bowed before me in all the mock splendor and puffed-up self-importance of their mission. They guaranteed that once they had found this Messiah I would be the first to know.

And I was foolish enough to believe them. My kindness was an error. I thought my flattery and favors would be enough to draw them back again, but the days passed and no word came.

Then I flew into a rage. What ignominy was this? Tricked by a few addled travelers; made to eat my words in front of courtiers and staff. I slammed my fists upon the table. 'Why weren't they followed?' I demanded. But the reason was obvious: I had never given the order. As I say, the exercise of power is a lonely thing.

So now the trap was sprung and the bait taken and the prey dispersed and probably warned—and me left staring into space, eluded. Made to look stupid. Made to look weak. I stamped around the palace and my rage was legion. This little king of Bethlehem was not going to defeat me. And these three kings from the east, they were not going to confound me. How could I, King Herod of Judea, true King of the Jews, descendant of David, have been so innocent as not to see that even while they drank my wine and slept in my sheets they had already given allegiance to this child? And they from a foreign land and owing him nothing. It should have been obvious. I should have taken account of their cunning and not just trusted my own.

For now I come to think of it, their allegiance—the allegiance of three foreigners—is the most troubling aspect of this whole episode. For if they will travel many miles, and risk their necks and come to other kingdoms to see this king, then who else might bow the knee before him? This child, if he is allowed to be more than a child, will too easily upset the equilibrium of our already-far-too-volatile nation. Our land occupied by the Romans. Our way of life and our privileges and our religious freedom, already threatened. Too many religious fanatics and would-be revolutionaries more than eager to believe in a new king: mad enough, given the opportunity, to even rally around a child. The danger was all-too clear. I had been aware of it from the moment of their arrival, but now I saw it with startling clarity. The stability of our nation and my own power and our future were threatened by this child. Something had to be done. If the fruit is poisonous then the bud must be nipped, however beautiful the flower.

So I began to plan. After all, that is how order is maintained. You must anticipate a threat. Stamp out the spark that crackles in the dry grass before all your barns are ablaze.

So it might not catch? Is that a risk worth taking? Much better to act swiftly and decisively, so that a whole harvest is saved. I therefore knew, almost in an instant, what I must do. The news and possibility of this little king had to be snuffed out. As I say, the exercise of power is not an easy thing.

I called my generals and chief of staff. We laid the charts upon a table and drew a circle wide around Bethlehem, a radius of many miles. Then I gave them their orders. Every boy child under two must be killed. It would be simple, merciless and precise. One painful cull and the problem solved.

So why am I still awake at this dark hour of the night? Why does sleep elude me? Why, when I do sleep, do I hear screaming in my dreams?

I have turned my decisions over. I have looked at the situation from every angle; not least I have taken a future perspective. I have looked at these events from the standpoint of history. So what if this Jesus had lived? What good would it have done, even if people had believed him a messiah? What if people had followed him? What if he had even come to Jerusalem itself and entered as a king, riding on a donkey as our prophet Zechariah had foretold? Well, any of us can read the prophets! Play-acting for effect is always the preoccupation of cunning minds, and impresses the masses who would rather believe in God's intervention than human artifice.

He would have been tracked down. That is the plain truth of it. He would have been destroyed. We would not have allowed it. And the Romans certainly wouldn't have allowed it. And on the way, who knows how many lives would have been mucked up? Gullible people will always be gullible. They are constantly on the lookout for messiahs. They will always follow, and in following they will die. How else do you think I recruit armies? How else do messiahs ply their

trade? So the answer was simple. Do now, swiftly and diligently, what would only happen later. And yes, others, innocent others, were caught up in it, and that is regrettable. But
in the end, from the longer point of view, it is expedient.

There is a band of pale pink light on the horizon. The dawn
of another day: the endless circle of days and the lonely exercise of power. My conscience is clear. I did what I had to do to
maintain order, to secure power, so that order can be maintained. Those deaths, and certainly his death, will be forgotten. Other babies will be born, and little lives will keep on
revolving just like the cycle of the days themselves. That is
the end of the matter.

Chapter 4

Casper

After Jesus was born in Bethlehem of Judea, wise men from the East came to Jerusalem, asking, 'Where is the child who has been born king of the Jews? For we observed his star at its rising, and have come to pay him homage.' ... When they saw that the star had stopped, they were overwhelmed with joy. On entering the house, they saw the child with Mary his mother; and they knelt down and paid him homage. Then, opening their treasure-chests, they offered him gifts of gold, frankincense, and myrrh. And having been warned in a dream not to return to Herod, they left for their own country by another road.

Matthew 2.1–2, 10–12

Casper

I am a stargazer. I have always had my head in the clouds.

When I was a boy I used to lie on the flat roof of our house and gaze at the stars. I would stretch out my arms and legs as wide as they would go so that I too might be a star, and that they might gaze at me. My mother called me a dreamer. She couldn't understand the patterns of the night sky, did not even know there was anything to be read in their gently changing constellations. But it is the moon that marks the months and pulls the tides. It is the stars that direct the traveler. On a stormy night, when the fierce waves billow and surge, the sailor has nothing else to lean on.

I have come to this conclusion. The darkness is my friend. For in the night the stars come out to shine and guide.

Most people learn to look down. Not me. I would not let my horizon shift. So there are obstacles in the path? Let them trip me up. Better to keep looking upwards, to chase after dreams and stumble, than only ever see the few steps in front of you and spend a lifetime going around in circles, getting nowhere fast. That is me: a dream-chaser, a stargazer, a misfit and a seer, a student of the cosmos and the galaxies. But I was also cautious. I liked to look at the stars and interpret their movements.

But I did not follow them myself. It was easier to advise others. And my wisdom was valuable. People would seek me out. My fluency in the stars made me a trusted navigator in the affairs of men. Admirals, politicians, governors and kings, those who wanted direction turned to me. But I never traveled myself. I became one who counseled the mighty and directed the strong. I knew how to get to the ends of the earth. But I stayed in my own chambers and drew the charts that others would follow.

But I never lost the art of gazing. The little boy who climbed onto roofs and stared at stars and dreamed of where they led was still alive in me. My dilemma was this: everything I had ever learned had come from contemplation. But I had never learned to act.

So when I saw a new star rising, I knew that it was my chance to change, my chance to follow, to awaken the dream inside me. For this star had to mean something. It had to lead somewhere. And so I set out. Not very well prepared for travel, but with servants to help me and a purse on my belt, I took to the road.

It was a joyous thing to be moving, to be actually doing something rather than just plotting a course for others. Things happen on the road. All sorts of encounters and adventures. There were other travelers too. Stargazers like me who searched the sky to see what promises it held. We found each other. We looked into the mirror of our own histories and saw a congruence of mind and will, and we banded together for conversation and for protection and for the simple pleasures of companionship and common purpose. When everyone else was safe in bed, we were on the road, moving westwards, following the star. It was a hard journey, and a cold coming we had of it. There were some who made us welcome. But there were many more who feared the stranger, especially ones whose bearing seemed to suggest wealth and power. What armies may trail in their wake? And there were bandits, and barren lands, and cold, cold nights.

We only made one mistake. And it was nearly fatal. At the last step we broke the habit of a lifetime and looked down. We suddenly trusted our own charts more than the star that had led us so patiently. We allowed ourselves, for a moment, to be enticed by the wealth and power that we thought we had left behind, but perhaps were still seeking. After many months of journeying, we arrived in the troubled province of Palestine, and seeing the star settle went straight to the palace of the king. How foolish we were. How unsettled by the beguiling glamor and seductive spin of powerful men. Here was a man who could see no further than his own beautifully manicured hand. And we went to him! Someone whose strength was completely consumed with the necessity of holding onto what he had—and at all costs. We quickly saw through him, despite his pathetic efforts to ensnare us. But we knew that we were also in his hands, that he would use us. For he only wanted to hear what he needed in order to subvert and control. There is nothing more dangerous than a weak man with too much power. I don't suppose he has ever looked upwards in his life. Sleeping on his sumptuous mattress, wrapped in the extravagance of silk, that was my most uncomfortable night in years. So when we left in the morning we quickly resolved never to return, and thankful for the word of his ancient prophecy we made our way to Bethlehem.

Oh, how the order of the universe changes. In the chill twilight of a winter's day we arrived in the town where the star rested. It didn't take many inquiries to find that there was indeed a mother and a newborn son. Behind the inn, at the edge of the town, was an outhouse, not much more than a stable, but sheltered from the rain and from the worst of the east wind that blew across the plain. We knocked on the door, feeling both excited and also vaguely stupid. What had we come to see? What was the purpose of our journey? We hardly knew. We were men compelled. Old men behaving like children, traveling on a whim with no particular destination in mind. Wise men, behaving like fools, believing that stars led somewhere.

A man about our age opened the door. He looked weary and wary. But there was a steadfast kindness in his eye that was also prepared to trust. He asked us our business, and even though we had come all this way believing that the star we followed presaged the birth of a king, to each of us, in that moment, it seemed very foolish. So we just said a child, we heard a child is born; we saw a star, we followed it; we don't know what it means, but it led us here. He opened the door to us. He opened wide his arms to us. He welcomed us in. And there, in a dark corner, wrapped in blankets and huddled against the cold and the clamor of the coming night, was the child, cradled in his mother's arms.

And whose heart is not lifted by such a sight? I don't mind telling you that my mind was whirring with all sorts of muddled and delighted thoughts. The tender beauty of the child and its mother, but also what we had left that morning.

Why was Herod so frightened of this child? Why had he been so keen for us to return, and to tell him where the child was? What threat to him was this? And what were those ancient prophecies that his councillors had so solemnly quoted? What did this child's birth mean?

We introduced ourselves. We went closer. We were tongue-tied and nervous. We didn't know whether to say everything or nothing. So we were silent for a while. Just looking. But we had brought gifts. Gifts for a king. They seemed somewhat out of place in the cramped squalor of these surroundings. At the same time we realized they were perfect. We were part of a drama so much bigger than ourselves; something we would probably never understand properly. We simply had to carry on faithfully playing our part.

We looked at each other, and without speaking rummaged in our bags to retrieve the gifts. Gold—for gold belongs to a king. Sweet-smelling incense from Mesopotamia—for a king is also a priest and one who intercedes with gods as well as men. And ointment of myrrh—for death and birth belong together, framing the life of every man. We laid the gifts before the still unstirring child. We smiled inanely and shrugged our shoulders, for even the expensive beauty of the precious things we had brought paled against the greater light of newborn life. After all, is there anything more beautiful in all the world? We saw it clearly that night, though we didn't know then how exceptional this beauty was to be.

Then the mother and father told us their own strange story. Our tongues were unshackled by it. We explained about the star and the traveling, but also of Herod and what we felt for sure were his murderous intentions. We talked into the night, then slept, huddled against our animals for warmth in the makeshift shelter of that outhouse.

In the middle of the night the baby stirred. It was a painful, plaintive cry, and for a few moments went unheeded. We lay in the blackness of the night listening to it. His mother woke. She quickly reached out to him. Her presence was reassurance. He was soothed by the warmth of her touch and the generous abundance of her breast. I saw his little fingers curl and grip his mother's thumb. And she stroked his cheek, and sang softly to him, a foreign song in words I did not know, but it was vast and beautiful, like a song sung in Eden itself.

It was the most common thing in the entire world: a new-born child. It was also the most beautiful. And somehow, in that moment, we knew that something special was unfolding before us. But we couldn't explain it. We had come looking for a birth, the birth of a king, and we had found a birth; we had found something momentous and lovely, but it didn't fit the categories that we had envisaged or expected. We had found a child—just a child—but one who already struck fear into the hearts of powerful men, and whose parents told fantastic stories of angels and shepherds, and of God visiting the earth. Jews do indeed believe strange things—they are famous for it—but this was stranger still. Not just one God, but one God come down to earth, one God sharing the life of men. Was this what the stars had led us to: the heavens themselves come down to earth?

As mother and child held each other and drifted back into sleep, I found I couldn't settle. Something was stirring me. I looked out through the gap in the door to the night sky. The stars were blazing in their intricate and myriad beauty. What did they mean? I no longer had any idea. I could read them and read them, but they would only lead back to the vanity of my own conclusions. So this is the question I am left with: what is wisdom? What does it actually mean to be wise? I thought it meant knowledge and information, the ability to work things out, speed of tongue and mind. I thought it meant ideas or even vision. These were concepts I was secure with, things I could return to if I wished. But they all seem empty now. To be able to name the stars and plot their courses through the sky, or read the scrolls handed down by those who came before us, weren't these just skills that some people have and other people learn, and wasn't it all by chance? All the wisdom of the world seemed vanity. Were my particular skills any better or any more valuable than the labors of human toil, to till the soil or carry water from the well? And at least these brought forth actual results, and were tangible in ways my labors could never match. Or the craftsman's endeavor? Was it better or worse than my knowledge of the sky and the seasons? I was filled with doubt and anguish then. I had traveled so as to put my knowledge into action, but had found my knowledge emptied out. Instead of a king, a child. And in that child, a glimpse of rare and uncomfortable beauty. In the restful and yet also troubling moments of that night, seeing the bonds of love between mother and child, I wondered if true wisdom might be this: to know what matters, and to rest secure in the peaceful affirmations of loving and of being loved.

When I did sleep, I dreamed. Terrible dreams of what hateful men would do to this child, and of how the horrors of the world rise up, and those who have been let down by love lash out at all that's lovely. I saw King Herod in my dream. I saw his thirst for vengeance and his terrible intent. And the dreams confirmed our own darkest suspicions. We needed to leave. And so did the family. We had to travel a different way, far from Herod's palace and over the mountains, on paths that could not be traced. We would cover the tracks of our traveling, but we knew that we would always bear the marks of this strange and beautiful meeting. The whole direction of our lives was changed.

We said our goodbyes in the harsh bitterness of the dawn. The road ahead of us will be treacherous and hard. But I tell you now, as we turn our faces away from Bethlehem, it doesn't feel like an ending. Something has begun here, something that is to do with love. I cannot tell you any more than that; strangest of all, there is nothing more to tell.

Chapter 5

———◆———

David

In that region there were shepherds living in the fields, keeping watch over their flock by night. Then an angel of the Lord stood before them, and the glory of the Lord shone around them, and they were terrified. But the angel said to them, 'Do not be afraid; for see—I am bringing you good news of great joy for all the people: to you is born this day in the city of David a Saviour, who is the Messiah, the Lord. This will be a sign for you: you will find a child wrapped in bands of cloth and lying in a manger.' And suddenly there was with the angel a multitude of the heavenly host, praising God and saying, 'Glory to God in the highest heaven, and on earth peace among those whom he favours!'

When the angels had left them and gone into heaven, the shepherds said to one another, 'Let us go now to Bethlehem and see this thing that has taken place, which the Lord has made known to us.' So they went with haste and found Mary and Joseph, and the child lying in the manger. When they saw this, they made known what had been told them about this child.

Luke 2.8–17

David

My mother's sense of humor was noteworthy and renowned. She named me after Israel's most famous shepherd, but there the resemblance ends. I am not a king, and never will be.

But this night something remarkable has happened. And I feel like a king.

It began the way all our nights begin. With liquor and laughter and bawdy jokes; and when Sarah from the inn walked home along the lane at the bottom of the field I ran down the hill, whooping and screaming, and lifted her skirts and gripped her buttocks. She feigned disgust and pushed me away, but her red face and the little teasing look in her eye said something else, and I thought to myself, I will go to her in the morning and hold her again and weigh the ample pleasure of her flesh. I returned to the sheep, dreaming of that visitation. And the other shepherds, for there was a little gang of us on nights like this, grinned and gestured rather too graphically what they would like to do with her. And we laughed again. And told stories of past conquests. We exaggerated and boasted like stupid men do on lonely nights. We passed the bottle from hand to hand. It offered a brief relief from boredom and cold. I took a deep swig of its harsh, amber liquid, a fiery brew of fermented corn. The dark would soon be upon us. We were full of bravado.

Then the waiting began. The jokes gave way to conversation and the conversation gave way to silence. And in the real dead hours of the night even the silence seems deeper and emptier than at other times.

I remember the first time I ever killed a lamb. It was Passover time, and my father showed me what to do, how to be deliberate and swift. Holding the little thing by its hind legs I cut its throat and heard the gasps of its last breath and saw how my father held open the jaws of the wound so that the blood would flow out easily. I felt horror and triumph. I felt like a man, but I also felt like a knave. The little lamb looked at me as its life closed. Something inside me was saying: why all this killing, why all this blood, what does it mean? What difference does it make? Can it be more than food?

In the deep silence of the night it feels like the lifeblood of the world has drained away.

But I am being melodramatic. There are noises. Sometimes a frightened lamb will bleat, and one of us will roam around the perimeter of the field and check our makeshift fences and look out for foxes and bears. And we shout to each other, just grunts of acknowledgment, that all is well and no assistance is required. Or else it will just be someone snoring as their body caves in to sleep, and someone else prodding them awake. Or sometimes the haunting hoot of an owl.

I didn't know what time it was. No sun to help me. I looked at the stars. No help there either. The more you looked, the more there seemed to be. I knew they were the very floor of heaven, but it seemed like they went back forever. Some men could read the stars and be directed by them, finding their way from place to place, maybe even telling the hours of the night. Not me. I had to look to the earth. Such is the lot of a poor man. You have to make a wage, and there is little time for dreaming or scheming or looking at the stars. Sheep are very stupid things. They require constant attention. They wander hither and thither. They follow whoever offers a lead and submit to everyone. The fragrance of wild parsley or a sprig of thyme will lead them over a cliff. They need taking care of; when one is lost someone needs to seek it out.

Then it happened. Out of nowhere and with such a sudden rush of dazzling brightness, it was as if a thousand bolts of lightning had exploded from the heavens at once and cut a swathe of light across the sky. It was like daytime, like noontime only brighter, and with such brightness came a dreadful clarity, like a thousand piercing shafts of light that could see between bone and marrow, between body and spirit, between flesh and blood. At first it was frightening. I mean terrifying. I was flooded with light. It was consuming me. I felt almost lifted into it. Then it was calm assurance: not a break with reality but the dawning of the first real day there had ever been. And a voice. I mean, I heard it as a voice, but it was not a voice like I'm speaking to you now; and nothing to see, like I can see you and you can see me, but not less real, more. And the voice spoke of glory and peace: glory to God in the highest heavens and peace to the earth. Or was it singing? Was it the sweetest, loveliest music you have ever heard? Was it one voice or the thousand voices of a heavenly choir?

And we were still afraid. I looked at my comrades as the light rushed around us and the music filled the air. There was fear and wonder in their eyes. I suppose mine were the same. But there was also a sort of reflected glory on their faces. An inner light that almost matched the brightness of the sky.

Angels, they were. I realized it then. A host of angels in the sky. Heavenly messengers, God's agents. Telling us something. Not just about God's glory in heaven, but God's peace on earth as well. And then a solemn declaration: 'To you is born this day in the city of David a Savior, who is the Messiah, the Lord. This will be a sign for you: you will find a child wrapped in bands of cloth and lying in a manger.'

Well, you've never seen anything like it after that. The whole sky was ablaze with glory. We tumbled down the hill like mad things. The light went as swiftly as it had come, and everything was back to normal—only normal would never be the same again. We had seen the heavens open. We had seen with our eyes what the prophets had barely glimpsed. And we, simple men: uneducated, unread, ignorant of the law and all its suffocations. Love God and love your neighbor. That is all I knew. What hope of heaven for me! But now, with the heavens themselves opened to me; open to ordinary men.

We rushed into Bethlehem. We wanted to see what had happened. We had to find this child. So we abandoned our few sheep. We arrived at the outhouse behind the pub laughing and panting; then, aware of the noise we were making, hushed each other up and brushed each other down. We hung about outside the door like nervous lovers on a first date.

And we grinned at each other like we had never smiled before.

Then another silence. But this time not the silence of something empty, something incapable of noise or life. It was the silence of contentment, of arriving, of being held in the arms of one who knows and loves, and where words are no longer necessary. What a noise those angels had made. How come the whole town hadn't heard it! But what a silence in that stable. The silence of loving and of being loved; of knowing and being known.

We went into the stable then. The door wasn't barred. It was open to us—and, I suppose, to the whole waiting world.

We went in and knelt down. That's all we did. Fools and idiots, who for no reason of personal merit or insight had just received the richest fortune. We knew this. And we didn't need to say anything. We saw the child, and the child's mother. We saw her husband. He stood between us and the child for a few moments, but as we were on our knees there was not much to be frightened of—we were hardly a threat, despite our rough appearance—so then he smiled and beckoned us forward. We shuffled across the floor on our knees. It must have been comical to watch. We must have looked a real sorry sight. But it felt right. This was not a place to stand; this felt a holy place—like when Moses saw that burning bush and took his shoes off. This was not a time to speak. Whatever it was that God wanted to say to us that night, he was saying it in the silence of a child born. All the noise and rejoicing of the angels was to lead us here, deep into the silence of God's presence.

And there we stayed. For what seemed like ages. Kneeling and staring and smiling. Then, because none of us can bear too much reality for too long, and love to tell a story and share a joke, we rose and shook each other's hands and introduced ourselves. There was laughter and tears. I don't know how to describe it. We all spoke at once, and our strange stories of angels in the sky directing us here seemed to confirm their strange story of an angel's direction and the message that this child was from God. And though I don't pretend to understand why God would visit us here, in this way, in this dismal place, I can't deny that there was something magical in this night that words can't contain. Even as I tell you what the angels sang and how the sky was filled with light, it seems in part like someone else's life, or a story made up to emphasize that what happened was fantastic. All I know, and what I am left with, is the child: his silence and his presence and the adoration of his mother and the tenderness of love given and received.

Many words were spoken that night. When we left the stable as the new day dawned we were rejoicing—more drunk than any liquor had ever made us. We talked about it to everyone we saw. We shouted it out. We said a king was born, a messiah. And they laughed and winked and patted us on the back and got on with their lives like nothing had changed. Even the crabby old woman who runs the inn opened her door a fraction to glare at us. 'Peace on earth,' we said to her, laughing. 'A new king is born, here in Bethlehem.'

Who listens to a shepherd if he is not King David? Who listens to a child when a child cannot even speak, but only sleep and cry? And if this child is king, how will anyone know? Will he be like David and lead an army to victory, and kick out the Romans, and establish an empire? I can't see it. Not in this manger where he lies at the moment. This is a different sort of king.

But what do I know? A shepherd, an outcast: a dreamer of smutty dreams and cheap thoughts, a lover of wine and generous women? How can I know the mysteries of God? Or what God is saying through this child? But I do know this, and I will hold on to it, even if no one believes me, and even if I have to keep it to myself forever: a word was spoken tonight, but as the night turned into day I realized that it was not the words of the angels, nor our excited words of greeting, nor even the astonishing obedience of a mother who endured all the misunderstandings and the hardships that had brought her to give birth in a barn. It was the word of God: God's word spoken in the life of a child.

Chapter 6

Martha

In those days a decree went out from Emperor Augustus that all the world should be registered. This was the first registration and was taken while Quirinius was governor of Syria. All went to their own towns to be registered. Joseph also went from the town of Nazareth in Galilee to Judea, to the city of David called Bethlehem, because he was descended from the house and family of David. He went to be registered with Mary, to whom he was engaged and who was expecting a child. While they were there, the time came for her to deliver her child. And she gave birth to her firstborn son and wrapped him in bands of cloth, and laid him in a manger, because there was no place for them in the inn.

Luke 2.1–7

It's good to rest at last. It's been quite a night. If I had the energy I would get up and stoke the fire for some warmth, but all I can do is sit here and think about what's happened.

My feet are as sore and as swollen as a cow's udder after milking. I don't mind telling you that, my lovely. The fire will have to manage on its own.

Up all night, I've been. And I mean all night, right till now with the new day almost upon us. And I've a story to tell that in one way is the most ordinary story in all the world, another child born, another mouth to be fed, another turning of the world's endless cycle of being born and ending up dead—and I'm sorry if I sound cynical, but yes, I suppose I am a cynical woman—and at the same time a most fantastic, puzzling story, that I can't quite make sense of. That's why I can't sleep, I suppose.

So let me begin. Bethlehem. It's never been so crowded, nor business so good. That much I know. Quirinius, the crafty bugger, the governor, has called for a census to be taken and every man must return to the town of his birth to be registered, and then pay more tax into the bargain. Well, there's a lot been born here in Bethlehem. We are a fertile lot! Good hips. But there is little work here for an honest man, so those that were born here have also departed. Who could blame them! But now the town is heaving. They have had to return. So, good business for Quirinius, and good business for me as well, as it turns out. And those who have returned seem to have money in their pockets. Well, most of them, anyway. As I say, our business has been very good. Yes, very good indeed.

Anyway, where was I? Yes, last night. In the middle of the evening, about eight it was, with the inn at its busiest, everyone laughing and halfway drunk, a couple come to the door. He, older and serious and earnest-looking, and she, young and frightened and heavy with child. I mean *very* heavy with child. I mean about to drop her load at any moment. I smiled. Because I know that feeling. I've had seven children myself and the first is always fearful, and she such a slip of a girl, it was obvious to me that it was her first time. I didn't think the man was her husband—her father more like! But he was determined, and he wouldn't take no for an answer. And there was no room in the inn. I told him plain: there's no room, couldn't he see; the place was chock-a-block. Was he having a laugh, asking for a room at this time of the evening and with this many people in town? But he stood his ground. I like that in a man. So I folded my arms and smiled at him and stood my ground too. I told him there was no room. And he gestured towards the girl and told me what I already knew; and I told him that didn't change nothing, but if he insisted then they could go out the back. There was an outhouse, not much more than a cowshed, where the animals sheltered at night. It was warm and it was out of the wind. I would bring water and blankets for a small price.

And wine and bread as well if he was able to pay. Take it or leave it.

He looked at me for a long while. He was turning in it over in his head. He was desperate, but what I liked about him was he didn't show desperate. There was a dignity to him. He turned to her, the girl, Mary her name was, and explained the situation. She too had a crackle of fire in her eyes. She was tough. I like that. But she was also desperate. How could she not be? Anything is better than nothing, is what her face seemed to say, and neither of them had the time or the luxury to choose. They needed help.

My heart softened a bit then. I know I'm a hard woman. I'm prone to snap and ask questions afterwards. You have to be that way in this business. Who am I kidding? You have to be that way in this world. I have seen too much hardship and known too much grief to think anything else. But I suppose I also remember the hopes of a firstborn child—the dreams— though the prospects for this one are hardly promising. What a pair! This old fella and this young girl, far away from home in the dead chill of a winter's night and nowhere to rest their head.

'We'll take it,' he said.

I wiped my hands on the towel that was tied around my waist and gestured to the girl. 'Come here, my pretty,' I said. 'I've been this way before. When the time comes, nature takes over. You'll know what to do and I'll come and check on you if I can. Come this way.'

I led them round the back of the inn. The barn where our animals sheltered was no more than a rough covering of brush and hay propped against the overhang of the wall and shadowed on two sides by the large cypress trees that grew in the yard.

The animals were restless. They were not usually disturbed at this time of the evening. And it stank. There wasn't time to clean it out each day, and if we did bring in fresh straw it was in the morning. I felt another rush of pity for the girl then, and called to one of the servants to bring a bale of clean straw from inside. I pushed open the makeshift door of the shelter. I clapped my hands to get the animals—a cow, a couple of goats and a few scrawny chickens—to move out of the way. I made a corner of the stable as comfortable as I could, and when the fresh straw arrived made a seat for the girl and put the remainder of the straw into one of the feeding troughs. 'You can lay the child here when you need to sleep yourself,' I said.

Then her water broke. It just happened, and she stood there looking frightened and amazed. Her skirts were sodden, and she looked at me pleadingly, completely unprepared for what was about to happen next. Had her mother taught her nothing? She let out a whimper. The animals could sense something unfolding. They started banging their hooves against the ground and whinnying. Her husband looked away. He was useless. Men usually are. He just stood there staring hopefully at me. 'Come here,' I said to the girl. I held her then and felt the quick fluttering rhythm of her heart. She was scared. But also trusting.

'I've had seven children,' I told her. 'I'll help you with this one.'

And so I did. Through the long hours of her labor: through the choppy waters of strong and mounting contractions; through the calm waters of boredom and wondering if it will happen at all; through the screaming and the vomiting, when she cried out that she was too exhausted to go on, and when I myself started wondering if this child would ever be delivered; I sat with her. I held her hand. I wiped her brow. I told her stories of my own seven births. I felt between her legs to judge whether she was ready or not. After a few hours my husband came out. 'What pretty sight is this?' he muttered angrily. 'There are customers to be looked after and dishes to wash, you know.' Then he stomped back inside.

Her husband—Joseph, I gathered his name was—paced. He was what you might call a traditional father. He didn't actually do anything. He just kept muttering—or was he praying?—that all this was from God and was safe with God.

'Well, you're safe with me,' I told him. 'Now hold this cloth, and wipe her face when I tell you.'

In the darkest hour of the night, I suppose about two or three o'clock, the baby's head appeared. He stared, blinking and gawking at the world for what seemed an age. And she was crying out with the pain of it, and the great longing for the baby to be free. It was one of those strange halfway moments between the womb and the world, between what was and what is. Then with the next contraction, on a spasm of pain and joy, he was born.

I pulled him free and held him up for his mother to behold: a boy, all green and grey with the mucus of the womb and the effort of birth. I didn't need to spank him or pat his little back. The breath seemed to rush into him, and he filled his lungs and let out a loud, piercing cry. I laughed at him. 'Loud enough to wake the dead,' I said to his mother, 'or at least my sleeping tenants. He's a strong little fella.'

I laid him on his mother's breast. That was a beautiful moment. It always is. Tender. As old as the world itself. As new as the dawn. And she moved his little face to her breast, and he suckled there, and she held him and stroked his head. With the next contraction the placenta was delivered. I took the cord between my teeth and quickly bit it in two, and knotted the end. He was born, this baby. He was OK. He was well. And his mother too, she seemed fine. And even the husband was smiling now: relief as well as joy etched into his tired face. What a place for a baby to be born. What a couple.

Then she turned to me, the mother. 'His name is Jesus,' she said, and smiled at me.

Well, I thought that was the end of it and I could get to bed myself. As the girl slept, and as the child slept too, the husband picked him up and laid him in the clean straw in the manger that I had prepared. I told him that he should get some sleep as well. But I knew he wouldn't. His part had come, and he was happy to watch and wait. So now I'm back here, watching and waiting myself. You see, I can't sleep. This birth and this odd couple have touched my heart. The inn is quiet. Everyone else asleep. But I'm sitting here awake.

The fire has nearly gone out. There are a few embers just struggling to stay alight, fluttering and flashing but with nothing to feed on. If I get a few sticks and gently breathe upon them the fire will return. But not forever.

I don't know where these thoughts have come from. This fire burning low. A new fire kindled. Warmth, security, heat and light. I need them so much, and yet as I turn over the dying embers of my life—because that's how it seems to me, that's what I'm thinking about, all the beautiful things that are lost to me, all the hopes and dreams that have died in me—in the end it will all go cold and expire. Where is the fire and where is the light that will burn forever, radiant and unconsuming?

Now there is a commotion outside. A lot of noise. Probably some drunks. I open the door a fraction. It looks like the shepherds from the fields above Bethlehem. They are little more than vagrants. What mischief have they been up to? And have they been in there? Disturbing the baby? And what is it they are shouting about? A king born in Bethlehem? Peace to the world?

Then they are gone. Silence again. The emptiness of the night; and on the horizon the unhurried beginning of a new day as the approaching sunlight leaches slowly into the darkness.

What is going on? What has happened here this night? Who is this child that has visited me? Whose coming into the world have I shared? There is a strange and ominous fore-boding upon me. Also a spark of pure, uncompromised joy. Who isn't moved to wonder at the sight of a newborn child?

I turn back into the room. The fire is suddenly roaring. I watch the flames dance in the hearth. What has been kindled here?

Chapter 7

Joseph

Now the birth of Jesus the Messiah took place in this way. When his mother Mary had been engaged to Joseph, but before they lived together, she was found to be with child from the Holy Spirit. Her husband Joseph, being a righteous man and unwilling to expose her to public disgrace, planned to dismiss her quietly. But just when he had resolved to do this, an angel of the Lord appeared to him in a dream and said, 'Joseph, son of David, do not be afraid to take Mary as your wife, for the child conceived in her is from the Holy Spirit. She will bear a son, and you are to name him Jesus, for he will save his people from their sins.' All this took place to fulfil what had been spoken by the Lord through the prophet: 'Look, the virgin shall conceive and bear a son, and they shall name him Emmanuel', which means, 'God is with us.' When Joseph awoke from sleep, he did as the angel of the Lord commanded him; he took her as his wife.

Matthew 1.18–24

Joseph

I come from a long line of dreamers. You wouldn't know it to look at me. I am not what philosophers are supposed to look like: my hands are rough and gnarled from a lifetime at the lathe; knotty, like the wood I turn. But anyway, dreaming and philosophy is not the same thing. I don't question things to find out what they mean. I hope for things, so that inside this old body there is always a fresh spring rising.

I am a practical man. I make things. I take the hewn timber from the forest and I produce the chairs that you sit on, the tables you eat from, the beds you lie on. I know how to join one piece of wood to another. I know which wood works for which purpose. I know how to measure and how to saw. I know the value of a tool. I know that you don't mistreat them; that time spent cleaning and mending and sharpening is time saved from the job itself. I have the wisdom that the so-called learned will never know: a wisdom that comes from doing; and the satisfaction. When my work is done, it is done. There is no question, no turning back, no second thought. I do not ask whether a table is a chair if you sit upon it. But as I plane the surface down, work it till it is smooth and straight, I may dream who will sit at my table, and who will eat from it, and what delights they may share.

How could it be any other way? I was named after the most famous dreamer in history.

But life does funny things to you. All my dreams are still intact, but as the years have gone by they seemed to get buried deeper and deeper. There is that spring inside me, an underground stream that makes glad the heart, but I don't know whether anyone can see it anymore. Nobody calls me a dreamer, like they used to when I was young. Well, not till now. And until this year I felt the same about myself. I was alone. Self-sufficient but not fulfilled. Grafting, making ends meet, I inhabited the world like a single, solitary tree in the middle of a wide and empty plain.

But then it changed. Betrothal. Me an older man, and she a young girl full of joy and vigor; full of hope and expectation of what life could bring, full of zest. She reawoke my dreaming. After so many miles of traveling in the same direction, meeting her was like a turning in the road, a new possibility. It was arranged by our families, and none the worse for that, and the arrangements were made quickly so that we could get on with our life. I had had many dreams, but I had stopped dreaming of this. And her presence filled me with delight. She was a sudden burst of springtime joy in what felt like the long meandering decline of autumn. She was spring rains on thirsty ground, and her exuberance replenished the hidden springs of my own dreaming and flooded me. Her presence, and what it promised, irrigated me. There is no other way of putting it.

Was it love? I don't know. Not yet. Love isn't a feeling. Love isn't just desire, though how I desired her. Love is the patient accumulation of shared memories, the joining together of two lifetimes into one, the weaving of separate stories into this story. Love begins to grow when falling in love is left behind. It takes time. It matures slowly in the fertile ground of commitment, of determined choosing: this person and not another, this path and not that. Love isn't what men think it is. They mistake falling in love for being in love. They forget that the finest wines take many years to settle. They allow their eye to rove, and lose the greatest gift of all: a lifetime shared, to know and to be known.

That was what opened up for me when Mary became my intended. Hope blossomed. Love became a possibility, something to be started.

But no sooner had we begun, than things changed. And I have to tell you this tonight—with Bethlehem just a day's journey away and our traveling almost ended, and Mary, heavy with child nearing the completion of her time—I have dreams, and my dreams have given me faith that God is in this quandary that I face; but I have doubts as well: dark doubts and dark moments. Sometimes I find myself looking at Mary, looking at her body swelling with the life that is in her, and harboring dark thoughts that it is someone else's child she carries, and I am a fool to stand by her. After all, that's what everyone else says. They snigger behind my back, and say he is not so much a dreamer as a dupe. How could he be stupid enough to believe her tall tale, and why doesn't he just leave her to lie in the bed she has made; separate quietly, and let her stew in her shame?

And don't think I haven't lain awake night after night saying these same things to myself. You're a fool, Joseph, a stupid dreamer, a love-struck old man, and there is no fool like an old fool. You have been turned by the winsome smile of a pretty girl, and you are ready to believe anything. Except when I did sleep . . . after she first told me, and I saw the fear and horror in her eyes, the fear that I wouldn't believe her and wouldn't stand by her; and, yes, I was furious and angry and jealous, and all sorts of other things; I raged around the house and went into the yard at the back of my workshop and polished the blade of my axe and furiously hacked and chopped at limbs of timber till I was completely exhausted; but my fury still not spent, and then not able to sleep; not able to face her, not able to believe her, though still wanting to, seeing the pleading agony in her eyes . . . when I did fall asleep, I had a dream. A simple dream, no coded messages like my namesake, no starving cattle, no ripening sheaves, but a simple requirement. In the unfussy logic of a dream I was instructed clearly: 'Do not be afraid to take Mary as your wife. Do not abandon her. The child conceived in her is from the Holy Spirit. She will bear a son and you are to name him Jesus, for he will save his people from their sins.' And then the words from Isaiah the prophet that I had heard many times ran through my dream: 'Look, the virgin shall conceive and bear a son, and they shall name him Emmanuel, which means, 'God is with us.'

And what do you do with a dream like that? Ignore it? Despise it? Argue against it? I woke with a start. It was still night, and I had been asleep for only a few minutes. But the dream and what it said to me were as clear as the day. It was as if God himself had spoken to me, a simple practical man in the uncoded clarity of my dream, and asked me just to be faithful: faithful to Mary and faithful to the dream inside me.

I ran those two words over in my mind—*Jesus*, for he will save his people; *Emmanuel*, God is with us. Is this who the child will be? One who saves? God with us?

I was comforted and confused. What is it the psalm says? I have always loved that verse, when I go to the synagogue and hear the ancient prayers chanted, and the brooding resonance of the priest's deep baritone, and the clouds of incense mysteriously burning and rising like prayers to heaven: 'there is a river that makes glad the city of God'. Were those the streams stirring inside me? And also in Mary? Was she the city of God, the place where God has come to dwell?

And so I have done what I have been told. I lay on my bed for a few more hours, then I rose before dawn and walked the half mile or so to Mary's house. I knew she wouldn't be sleeping either; our two stories were already becoming one. Sure enough, even as I approached the house, I heard the sound of her gentle weeping. I think she had been up all night too, worrying and probably praying that there would be some sense in all of this. She opened the door to me and there was a lovely defiance in her eye. She was ready to meet whatever it was I would give her. I saw then, as clear as the dream, her own certainty in what was inside her. I held her tiny, soft hands in mine, looked her square in the eye, and told her that I was with her, that I believed her; I had had a dream, and my dream had confirmed her story.

I said no more. I am not a man of words, but deeds. I do what I believe to be right. I do not look back. I returned to my workshop. I tidied up. I arranged the chopped wood into a pile outside the door, ready for the fires of winter. I set about my daily work.

Others came to me. They came with every kind of advice and admonition. They believed all sorts of things about me, and about Mary. I said nothing. I told them I would stand by her.

We became the talk of the town. People would point and whisper and plot. But inside I knew. Or at least I thought I knew. Or at least I knew what I had decided. I knew how I had chosen to respond. And I was not going to go back on this. Something was unfolding in the shared story that was my life with Mary. God had visited her in some way that I will never fully understand. For even if you begin to believe the strangeness of the story I am telling you, Mary is not what you might think she is. She is not a quiet stream. She is a tempest. She is not an empty vessel, but a skin of wine uncorked. She is not what men think godly, self-effacing and discreet, reposed and receptive. She is a force: a force of joy and energy and life. And I love her for that. I will go on loving her for that. I will stand by her. And if it is so that God has chosen her to be the Mother of the Lord—and notice in these moments I still have to say 'if', for my faith is not that great—then surely he could have chosen someone better prepared, better positioned, and with more resources of maturity and wealth. What capital has she for this vocation, except the abundance of her love for life, for God, for the crazy possibilities that what she says an angel laid before her?

Now my head spins again. An angel? A messenger from God? And a message for this young, green Nazarene shoot, hardly broken through the earth, hardly flowered, no more than a girl, her life hardly started. How can this be?

Well, tomorrow we may know. We should be in Bethlehem by dusk and this baby can't be far from birth. I place my hands upon Mary's stomach each evening as we lie down to sleep, and I feel the baby's strong movements, turning in her womb and kicking out against the world.

But will I know then? God with us? What does a son of God look like, except a son of man, a child like every child? And for what purpose is this child born? Is it to save? How does that work? Who will know him and who will believe him?

Joseph

Night is falling and we must rest. There is a place here beneath the vast, protective canopy of an oak. It could have stood here for centuries. It is impossible to imagine it not being here, and yet I know (because I know the land and I know trees) that it too, like every life there is, was born of a miraculous and tiny beginning, just a seed in the earth.

I know the names of all the trees, and their habitat and their uses. In winter I can tell them by their shape, in summer by their leaf. Cedar, sycamore, oak and aspen; I know them all. Like Adam I can name them. I admire their strength, their steadfastness, their inscrutability. They gaze upon the world and do not blink. They grow accustomed to a single place. They put down roots. They don't long for distant horizons. They are satisfied.

How unlike us they are. We fidget to be different from others, or better; or idly long to be someone else, or somewhere else, or not a man at all, but a god. How petty and futile the world suddenly seems. What hope is there for all our falsehood? Idolatry was always our greatest failing—making God out of wood, rather than seeing God in the wood itself.

Mary is settling down for the night now. Although she is tired, so tired, she is still all focus and energy, holding and bearing an inner stillness and resolve that is beyond the meandering fantasies of most men. What tree is she? It must be a holly: prickly and evergreen and bearing in the midst of winter the brightest berry. And the child she bears, this child from God, what tree is he? I cannot know, but I imagine him a vine; that the uncorked, poured-out, full-measured vintage of Mary's challenging faithfulness is going to bring something wonderful to the world. Something refreshing.

Or will he be rejected? Will he be broken? Will he be a barren tree on a lonely hill that bears no fruit at all?

Chapter 8

Elizabeth

In the days of King Herod of Judea, there was a priest named Zechariah, who belonged to the priestly order of Abijah. His wife was a descendant of Aaron, and her name was Elizabeth. Both of them were righteous before God, living blamelessly according to all the commandments and regulations of the Lord. But they had no children, because Elizabeth was barren, and both were getting on in years.

Once when he was serving as priest before God and his section was on duty, he was chosen by lot, according to the custom of the priesthood, to enter the sanctuary of the Lord and offer incense. Now at the time of the incense-offering, the whole assembly of the people was praying outside. Then there appeared to him an angel of the Lord, standing at the right side of the altar of incense. When Zechariah saw him, he was terrified; and fear overwhelmed him. But the angel said to him, 'Do not be afraid, Zechariah, for your prayer has been heard. Your wife Elizabeth will bear you a son, and you will name him John. You will have joy and gladness, and many will rejoice at his birth, for he will be great in the sight of the Lord.' . . .

After those days his wife Elizabeth conceived, and for five months she remained in seclusion. She said, 'This is what the Lord has done for me when he looked favourably on me and took away the disgrace I have endured among my people.' . . .

In those days Mary set out and went with haste to a Judean town in the hill country, where she entered the house of Zechariah and greeted Elizabeth. When Elizabeth heard Mary's greeting, the child leapt in her womb. And Elizabeth was filled with the Holy Spirit and exclaimed with a loud cry, 'Blessed are you among women, and blessed is the fruit of your womb. And why has this happened to me, that the mother of my Lord comes to me? For as soon as I heard the sound of your greeting, the child in my womb leapt for joy. And blessed is she who believed that there would be a fulfilment of what was spoken to her by the Lord.'

Luke 1.5–15, 24–25, 39–45

I was always waiting in the wings. Always wondering when it would be my turn to go on. My sisters and my friends were cleverer than me, prettier than me, more confident than me. I was always waiting to be picked. My marriage has not been without love. But there hasn't been much joy. It just feels as if life has never really got started. And I have stored up regret. I have spent too long saying 'if only'.

I don't blame Zechariah. He is a good man, a holy man, a godly man, a priest descended from Aaron. But he was embarrassed by it. And he was embarrassed by me. You know how men are; they can't talk about their shame. They bury themselves in their work. They look the other way. Everyone assumed it was my fault that we had no children. But it could have been his. Does anyone really know? We didn't talk about it. We just went our separate ways. Together, but not united. There was emptiness between us. The emptiness of the absent child we dreamed of, and a fulfilment that will not be.

When my friends got pregnant, I was pleased for them at first. 'It will be my turn soon,' I said. But nothing happened. And then, after a few years, nothing happened that would make anything happen, if you know what I mean. My sterility was more than an embarrassment. It was a curse. It was as if my body was laughing at me every month, flushing away the possibility of another life. I saw women heavy with child, some of them for a fourth or fifth or sixth time, and I was covetous and angry. I would hold the limp rolls of flesh that my stomach had become and ache with the empty disappointment of it all. Life hadn't really got started. I was a woman, a healthy woman, a healthy woman in her prime; but my womb was as dry as a riverbed in a drought, and my sagging breasts as empty as the grave. There was life in me; but it was on hold. There were possibilities in me, but they never came to anything.

I retreated into myself. I was a good wife, in the sense that I did as my husband bade me: I cared for him, I kept the house proudly and diligently. But it was all a charade. Inside, I was stewing with disappointment and envy. It was eating me up, gnawing into my womb, mocking its barrenness, filling me with bile. But even this never came out. I was like a kettle of water that simmers on the edge of boiling. But I never hissed. I never spilled over. I never embarrassed anyone. I never told them how I felt. I never lived. Mine was the shadow of a life. I perfected the contented smile that hid the rage and sadness. But that didn't prevent people's pity. They would wait till I had passed them on the street, and then whisper their torrid suppositions. They knew I was barren. And they enjoyed speculating why. Whose sin and whose failing had caused this emptiness?

It affected my dreams. I stopped hoping for anything. Hope had only let me down. I would just get through each day. And at night I would retreat to the safety of childhood where I could still, just about, remember a time when hope existed, and when I thought life would be good; a time when I thought, I will have my turn, I will be loved and I will love in return; I will fill my quiver with sons, and teach my daughters the joys of hearth and home. But there were no joys. Just each day passing, each day fading into the next, the endless cycle of day and night, waking and sleeping, and the dawning realization that it would never be different.

Until the day it was. And even then, me an old woman bearing a child, there is a kind of mockery to it. This is not how it is meant to be. Don't get me wrong. I am pleased, so pleased, so overjoyed that there is a child growing within me; but why now? And who is this child? And how is it that my dry womb and my dry breasts are now so filled with bursting energy and life?

It happened on the day that Zechariah was serving in the sanctuary. As I say, he is a priest. This is what he does. His section was on duty, and as is the custom, someone was chosen to make the offering of incense, and the lot fell to him. Now at the time the whole assembly of the people was praying outside. Zechariah went inside the sanctuary, he was making the offering, when—and I know this sounds crazy—an angel appeared to him, standing bolt upright before him at the right side of the altar of incense. When Zechariah saw the angel, he was terrified; and fear overwhelmed him. But the angel said to him, 'Do not be afraid, Zechariah, for your prayer has been heard. Your wife Elizabeth will bear you a son, and you will name him John. You will have joy and gladness, and many will rejoice at his birth, for he will be great in the sight of the Lord.' And the angel went on: 'He must never drink wine or strong drink; even before his birth he will be filled with the Holy Spirit. He will turn many of the people of Israel to the Lord their God. With the spirit and power of Elijah he will go before him, to turn the hearts of parents to their children, and the disobedient to the wisdom of the righteous, to make ready a people prepared for the Lord.'

But Zechariah—like me, I suppose—was filled with doubt as well as fear. After all, that's what age and disappointment does to you. It makes you cynical. It makes you suspicious of joy. So he says to the angel: 'How will I know that this is so? For I am an old man, and my wife is getting on in years.' And he was only speaking the plain truth: me an old woman, him an old man; and years of disappointment behind us. But the angel replied, 'I am Gabriel. I stand in the presence of God, and I have been sent to speak to you and to bring you this good news. But now, because you do not believe my words, which will be fulfilled in their time, you will become mute, unable to speak, until the day these things occur.'

And that was what happened. The people were waiting outside the sanctuary, wondering what on earth was happening. And when Zechariah does at last appear, he has been struck dumb. He gestures to them, but he can't speak. And they realize that he has seen a vision. Or at least they think they realize. In my opinion, those crowds are always a smidgeon too eager to believe that God has spoken, or angels have visited. But this is the plain truth of it. I am pregnant. You can't argue with it. As I sit on my porch scanning the horizon, waiting for my cousin to come, the baby is kicking inside me.

When his time of service ended, Zechariah came home. Of course, he couldn't speak to me either. But almost straight away I felt different. I knew something had changed. In those next few weeks, my body started changing. I hid myself away. For five months I saw no one. But then, when I was sure, when there was no mistaking it, when my belly was as round and as proud as any mother to be, I told it plain; I showed the world: 'This is what the Lord has done for me when he looked favourably on me and took away the disgrace I have endured among my people.'

And here she comes: Mary, my cousin. How do the Scriptures put it?—leaping upon the mountains, bounding over the hills like a young gazelle. She is a bundle of joy and energy. She is a force. She also bears a child in her womb. She also has a strange story to tell. I watch her coming and I see in her youthful exhilaration what I could have been. But I am not envious. The passing years, and this sudden influx of life, have not made me bitter. Like the lengthening shadows of the evening, there is a sadness in me, but also a growing recognition and a joy that somehow I am being used for the purpose of God, and that my child, like Elijah, directs the heart to God.

But where is God in this encounter? For as Mary arrives, standing before me like the rose of Sharon, like a lily among brambles, flushed, confident, exultant, fabulously alive, the child in my womb leaps. It is as if the unborn child in me recognizes and greets the unborn child in her. There is a movement, and it is of the Spirit of God; for, dare I say it, God is here. I know it, but I don't know how I know it. God is come with Mary, in her womb, and my child knows it. And I shout out with joy, with the first searing flush of joy; and as I say them, the words cast away the agonies of a lifetime: 'Blessed are you among women,' I say to Mary, 'and blessed is the fruit of your womb.'

And Mary looks at me. We stand there on my porch. The afternoon sun beats upon us. We are both breathing heavily. She is tired from her walking, but also elated, jubilant. And I am like one reborn. The child within me has seen and done something that seems to say that everything is changed. There is a new song in the air. And I say to Mary, perplexed, but very, very happy, 'Why has this happened to me, that the mother of my Lord comes to me? For as soon as I heard the sound of your greeting, the child in my womb leapt for joy. And blessed is she who believed that there would be a fulfilment of what was spoken to her by the Lord.'

Then we embrace. We laugh and we shout out loud. We punch the air. We raise our hands in celebration. We cannot yet hear the music of this new song, but its words are forming in our mouths, and for Mary, suddenly, it is on her lips: a new way of looking at the world, a new way of inhabiting life. 'My soul magnifies the Lord,' she cries out. 'My spirit rejoices in God my Saviour. He has looked with favour on the lowliness of his servant. All generations will call me blessed. The Mighty One has done great things for me, and holy is his name. His mercy is for those who fear him from generation to generation. He has shown strength with his arm. He has scattered the proud. He has brought down the powerful. He has lifted up the lowly. He has filled the hungry. He has sent the rich away empty. He has helped his servant Israel, in remembrance of his mercy, according to the promise he made to our ancestors, to Abraham and to his descendants for ever.'

Now it is evening. Mary sleeps and I watch. Darkness falls, but it is no longer dark.

There is fire in my belly. Hidden in the darkness of my womb, and of Mary's womb, there is life and light. I stroke my swollen stomach. Six months. Only three more to go. The child isn't leaping anymore, but turning slowly. I feel his gentle movement inside me. God has helped his servant Israel. He has remembered his mercy. He has made good his promise. My child points to Mary's child. My child prepares the way for her child. I don't understand it, but the evidence that God is here is plain within us and between us. There is music in the air. Lights are being kindled. A fire is burning, and it will not be put out.

Chapter 9

---·---

Mary

In the sixth month the angel Gabriel was sent by God to a town in Galilee called Nazareth, to a virgin engaged to a man whose name was Joseph, of the house of David. The virgin's name was Mary. And he came to her and said, 'Greetings, favoured one! The Lord is with you.' But she was much perplexed by his words and pondered what sort of greeting this might be. The angel said to her, 'Do not be afraid, Mary, for you have found favour with God. And now, you will conceive in your womb and bear a son, and you will name him Jesus. He will be great, and will be called the Son of the Most High, and the Lord God will give to him the throne of his ancestor David. He will reign over the house of Jacob for ever, and of his kingdom there will be no end.' Mary said to the angel, 'How can this be, since I am a virgin?' The angel said to her, 'The Holy Spirit will come upon you, and the power of the Most High will overshadow you; therefore the child to be born will be holy; he will be called Son of God. And now, your relative Elizabeth in her old age has also conceived a son; and this is the sixth month for her who was said to be barren. For nothing will be impossible with God.' Then Mary said, 'Here am I, the servant of the Lord; let it be with me according to your word.' Then the angel departed from her.

Luke 1.26–38

Mary

My fondest memories are of home. Here in the hour of the evening breeze, with the last rays of the dipping sun shining upon me, I rest in them; curled up in my mother's arms at the end of the day, I remember her singing to me, and telling me stories from the Scriptures. I remember the sweetness of her voice, and the stability of her gaze. She was always preparing me, teaching me about life, showing me the way to go, helping me to become a woman. She taught me the names of the flowers and the trees—which to eat and which to avoid— how to till the soil, how to bake and mend. I helped her around the house, preparing for that day—that day soon— when I too will keep a household going.

I think I always loved the world; and loved life; and loved the plants and creatures upon it. I have always believed in it, and seen God in it. I love to hear the Scriptures, especially the psalms, but also proverbs and prophets, and the dark, stirring beauty of Solomon's song. For I too know such passion. It burns within me, a fire that cannot be put out.

My mother also thought me a little wild. 'Finding a husband won't be easy,' she used to say with a smile. Like a young and strong-willed filly, she and my father didn't think I could be easily tamed. But they were wrong. I just wanted a strong love, and a deep passion, and a way to channel this energy and faith and knowledge of God which was boiling inside me.

This is how I see it. This is my creed. I believe in the flowers that brighten the world and give the earth its springtime dress: the chamomile that grows in the yard, the oleanders that flourish in the streams, the sage and hyssop, the tiny white iris and the milk vetch; and at this time of year, the tall, bright blue lupins. They say the lupin is the oldest plant of all; that it grew in Eden itself.

And I believe in the flowers that bloom in the dark of winter as well as in the spring. Here in Galilee, the anemones are mostly red. They are like great drops of blood splattered upon a frozen earth. They start to appear in late December. They rise from the cold death of winter. But when it is wet, like it has been this year, they continue to splash their color across even the dry hills to the east until the end of March and into April. This year, strangely and beautifully, they have overlapped with the poppies. Both are big and bright and red and spread colorfully over all the land. It is easy to confuse them, but the poppies are bigger, and their flowers have just two petals with a large blotch at the bottom, while the anemone has six petals radiating out from a cluster of small purple stalks in the middle. The anemone, like most winter flowers, grows from a bulb; the poppy grows from a tiny seed, almost as small as mustard, and easily scattered on the wind. That is why we find poppies everywhere. And the seeds are good to eat. You can sprinkle them on bread. They make a good tonic for animals, and the fruits, the hard seedpod that is left after the petals have fallen away, can be used in an infusion that is good for coughs. The petals can be used to make ink.

Mary

I believe in the orchids, most handsome of all. They are rare and mysterious. They seem to mirror the animals that live among them: butterflies, bees, spiders, even lizards. And near Jerusalem, where the purple-toothed orchid is quite common, the tubers are ground into a paste and make an enchanting drink. Capers also grow there: a shrub with large white and yellow flowers and long, red, delicate stamens. The flower buds are delicious pickled. You can eat the leaves raw as a salad. Their flavor is sharp and clean. You see them thriving abundantly, growing out of the tiniest crack in the walls of the Temple itself.

And I believe in the trees: massive evergreen cypress trees, and lofty cedars and oak. I love to climb them, and sit high up in their branches, and gaze from them at the immensity of the world, or lie beneath them and stare up at their towering majesty. I believe in the acacia, whose branches are armed with spines; and the evergreen carob and the locust tree whose seed pods can be as long as a span and are filled with a sticky pulp and a syrup that is as sweet as honey.

On the plains there are palm trees. The gardens of the wealthy have olive and fig trees, even apricot, pomegranate, almond, pistachio and walnut from Persia. Sometimes the fruits fall on the wrong side of the wall and you can gather them in your apron and enjoy their succulent splendor.

And I believe in the birds: the swifts that return in the spring; the owls that watch through the night; the sparrows that peck around the yard. And the animals: the branded newts, the yellow salamanders, the toads and marsh frogs, the squirrels, the honey bee, even the scorpion. All of it. I believe in it. I see it and inhabit it and learn its ways. It is a world of precision and beauty.

And I believe in the seasons: the fertile promise of spring, the hot, sultry abundance of the summer, the cool, warm, wet golds and yellows of autumn, and even the more brutal beauty of the winter cold. Each has its place, and each its purpose. The tree in winter is no less alive than the tree in spring. Its energy is amassing beneath the earth; it gathers itself to itself, ready to burst from the grave and fill the world with color and plenty. The mustard seed is the smallest seed of all. Yet it grows to such height and breadth that the birds of the air shelter in its branches.

And there are seasons to life: the exuberance of youth and the responsibilities of age. Then there are moments within seasons, where one thing that wasn't, suddenly is, bursting it seems from nowhere, but actually part of what always was and what always will be. Like the birds that leave us when the days grow cold and brief, but return in the spring and build their nests where nests have always been built, and feed their young with the insects and flowers which also return at just the right time. So there is a wonderful symmetry to the span of the seasons and to the pattern of a lifetime and the meaning of each moment within it. As the Scriptures say, 'From whose womb did the ice come forth, and who has given birth to the hoar-frost of heaven? . . . Who has put wisdom in the inward parts, or given understanding to the mind?"*

I believe in God. I have this tremendous sense of the presence of God. Sometimes it frightens me, because I don't know what to do with it; I don't know where it came from. I know that other people don't see it or feel it quite like me. It's not that they don't believe, but belief does not seem to infuse them and inspire them, like it does me. And it is not a belief that drives me to the synagogue, or even to the Scriptures, though I love both, and wish I could read the Scriptures for myself; it is a belief that propels me deeper into the world, and gives me a joyful longing to embrace the world and try to make it how God wants. I simply believe in God like I believe in the flowers and the trees and the birds and the seasons. God is there, with me and for me.

God is fact for me. But not a fact like other facts; I know that. Believing is not knowledge. It is not the same as knowing the flowers and the trees, or knowing the pattern of the seasons or the leading of the stars. I believe in God because God is. God is in the world, but God is not part of the world. Nor is God merely an explanation for the world. God is not a plug to fill a gap where other knowledge fails or falls short. God is not a prop to bolster feeble thinking. God is not a thing. You cannot say, here is God, or there is God. God is not a shadow upon

---

* Job 38.29, 36.

the world that you might miss if you were looking the wrong way. I believe in God, and God is the lens through which I look upon everything and receive everything. And because of it, my life, and my experience of the world, is magnified. I am filled and overflowing with a wild joy. I burn with passion to ravish and enjoy this life, and see the world become truly what it is meant to be, when it tunes itself to God, and sees and enjoys the world like God enjoyed it on that very first Sabbath. Believing is trusting that God is and that God will be.

For God is the beginning. God is the ever-present and sustaining source of sunlight and cyclamen, of dewdrop and daisy, of heartbreak and heartbeat.

God is the end. I look into the myriad multitude of the stars that shine like radiant beams of florid hopefulness, pinholes into heaven itself, and see that as God is my origin and the meaning to each day and each moment, so God will be my ending. I do not need to describe it or explain it, and even if I did it cannot be so reduced. But I do believe it. It is my pulse. It is simply this: my life is an offering of praise to the wonderful God who made life possible.

My breath—this breath, which I feel drawing into my lungs now—is breath of heaven, breath of God, pure gift: God himself breathing into me and making my life possible, making what seems impossible apparent, for the dust of this earth is charged with astonishing fertility. And while I know that most men are too busy with their toil or their silly lusts to sing out praise, that is what I want my life to be: a hymn of praise to God, to the God I see and know but cannot constrain or define. God is all energy, all joy and all majesty. You cannot pin God down. You cannot nail him, and say, this is God, this is where God is. He will rise up. He will rise up in the world he has made and in the people who know him. And that is my gift.

I see it today like never before. My gift is to know God. To be content in his presence by being content in the world, by walking softly and joyfully upon the earth, and knowing God by knowing the good of the good earth God has made and the wonders of the life he has given us. It is a thrilling thing to be seized and held by the presence of the living God.

Listening to me say this, you might think me mad, or holy, or deeply religious, or all three; but the truth is, I am just a girl: a happy, energetic, excited girl who is in love with life and all its possibilities, who wants to know how the world works, all its intricacies and all its benefits. I want to seize hold of life and all its possibilities. I want to enjoy it. I want to live every moment like it is the only moment I will ever have. I want to delight in the fantastic and beautiful variety of the world. I want to be passionate. I want to know love. I want to feel its hot breath upon me. I want to live.

Sometimes, when my work is done, and on a summer evening when I have time to myself, I like to escape into the hills and run and run till I can run no more. I love the feeling of the earth beneath my feet. I love it when my limbs are so tired that every muscle aches—that feeling when my body is completely spent. Then, lying beneath the trees, and watching the shadows lengthen, and smelling the musky fragrance of the perfumed flowers, it is all joy, all beauty.

Or like this morning, to go to the water's edge, to see the dawning heat of the sun disperse the mists that hang upon the water. To see the water's early morning milky flatness; to see it so still it is almost solid, and feel like you could walk upon it.

Oh, how I wanted to throw myself into those waters, to be cleansed and washed and born again. Or be a little girl once more, fetching water for my mother, dipping my pail into the well, waiting with expectation. It is a thrilling thing to be alive, to walk upon the earth, to taste its magnificence.

So, now I will tell you. Tell you how that which cannot be seen, but is more real than the trees and the mountains, is their source and their ending, is come to us; is come to us so that all may see, and that things unknown and hidden may be brought into light.

It is through me.

I say it with calm assurance, like I might tell you there is food on the table or a stranger at the door; and yet if you placed your hand upon my breast you would feel my heart beating faster than a falcon's wings as it hovers over a kill. I am the Lord's handmaid. He has come to me, so that through me God may be known.

This is how it happened, though I cannot give you an explanation. I can only tell you the story.

I was alone in the house. It was still early, the morning mists just cleared. I looked from the window and saw the sheep grazing in the fields, the newborn lambs playing among them. I couldn't see the shepherd. I looked for him. I was worried for the sheep, and especially for the lambs. Where could he be? Then I looked back into the house. I don't know why. Something was drawing me.

And there he was. Not the shepherd; not God himself, who cannot be looked upon—or can he? Will it now be so?—but someone. And this someone says to me plainly: 'Greetings, favoured one! The Lord is with you.'

Standing there, I don't know what I'm seeing, or what it means. This someone is 'a someone'. Someone I could reach out and touch, but not a person like I am a person. Suddenly I feel terribly cold; like my heart has been plunged into ice, my whole living suspended. And I am frightened. I know the Lord is with me. I know that already. I know it every day and every moment. So how else can he come to me? What is this stranger bringing? Where does he come from?

Silence. Then overhead, a bird sings. It is a beautiful, chirruping song, a song of undiluted joy: the song a bird sings when it builds its nest and prepares to welcome its young.

The stranger speaks again. There is warmth and comfort in his voice, though still not enough to stop me shivering in his presence. 'Do not be afraid, Mary,' he says. 'You have found favour with God. And now, you will conceive in your womb and bear a son, and you will name him Jesus. He will be great, and will be called the Son of the Most High, and the Lord God will give to him the throne of his ancestor David. He will reign over the house of Jacob for ever, and of his kingdom there will be no end.'

Another silence. I breathe it in, the import of his words. It is utterly fantastic. Unimaginable. He has finished speaking, and I don't know how to respond or what to say. Is this person a messenger from God? An angel? And how can this be? How can any of this be? For I am still a girl. Yes, betrothed to Joseph, a man I hope I may come to love, but not a man I have *yet* loved, or *yet* known. I am still a virgin. I have not dishonored myself, or him. What is happening here?

So I laugh. I laugh out loud and break the silence with a howl of protest: 'How can this be? This is madness. I mean, how can this be? I am still a virgin. I have not known a man.'

But it is not madness. The angel replies—for it is an angel, I see it now: a messenger from God sent to me, a wild, unruly and faith-filled girl from Nazareth. His voice is replete with a terrible certainty, as though what he is saying is what was always meant to be said, and is as plain and as true as the sun in the sky or the fire in the hearth: 'The Holy Spirit will come upon you, and the power of the Most High will overshadow you; therefore the child to be born will be holy; he will be called Son of God. And now, your relative Elizabeth in her old age has also conceived a son; and this is the sixth month for her who was said to be barren. For nothing will be impossible with God.'

This time the silence is complete. No bird sings. Not even a murmur of breeze whispers through the room. I breathe in, and I breathe out. But my breath is as quiet as the night. Oh, the night, how it feels like the night in that moment; and how glorious the coming dawn if I say yes.

My head spins. I am searching myself, digging deep into all that I have known about God and all I have known about the world. For this is a turning.

The angel looks away. Still there, but not so obviously there as before. Now you might find yourself looking beyond him, or even through him, and imagine yourself dreaming. Only, nothing has ever been as real as this. But it is a different reality: one that I cannot describe. It feels newly born. It is as if heaven has reached down to earth, and touched me. How silently, how silently, the wondrous gift is given.

Then I am not even trying to see the angel. I am looking to God; looking to God in the motes of dust that are illuminated by the bursting beams of sunlight flooding the room, revealing what was hidden; and looking for God in the spaces between them. For now there is a space in me that God is occupying, my welcome guest, my lover and my friend. 'Here I am,' I say to the wind and the sun, to the spots of dust and to the sky, and there is surprise in my voice that even I can hear, for something incredible is done in me. 'I am the servant of the Lord,' I declare to the world, though no one is listening. Not yet. 'Let what you have said,' I say to the angel, 'be done in me.' So God imparts to human hearts the wonders of heaven.

Let it be done in me according to God's word. Then, like a scroll rolled up, the angel is gone. Everything is as it was before, only everything is changed. I feel it deep within me and hold my stomach and try to imagine the life that is, even now, in that moment, dividing and dividing and coming into being inside me.

The world is changed. The cycle of the seasons and the cycle of life and death are changed. They continue on their way, but now there is a new music accompanying them. It is the song of heaven. The song of heaven come down to earth. The song of heaven being sung in me. God made visible, vocal, local, in the only way we could ever really see him: in flesh like our flesh, in flesh from my flesh, in the language of another human life.

Mary

It is far outside the usual pattern of things. I know that. Yet, even as I say these words, I know it is also the music of a new pattern, an incorruptible flesh, a fire that burns without consuming.

For now I can hold this to myself. I know what every pregnant mother knows: the fascinating secret of a life growing inside me. But it cannot be a secret for long.

And what will Joseph say? How will I explain it to him?

And what will the world say? And how will they ever know or believe that this child is from God?

What will they do to him?

I hold my arms tightly around myself. My heartbeat quickens. I feel a sharp pain—the first of many—for being a mother is a painful thing as well as thrilling. It feels horribly frightening and impossibly difficult. But the words of the angel beat within me: nothing is impossible with God. The Holy Spirit will come upon you. The power of the Most High will overshadow you. The child to be born in you will be holy; will be called Son of God.

And my cousin Elizabeth also pregnant. The shame that had driven her further into herself and deeper into the shadows of the world was ended. I knew then that I must go to her, and share this with her, and that we could support each other. There would be a way through, and I will treasure in my heart this story of what God has done—for me and for her. Now I see it clearly. I believe it. What is done in me is for everyone, so that all the world may see God. Elizabeth will be the first to receive it. Her darkness slipping away. Her shame expunged. She will be brought out into the light of day.

Jesus. I will call him Jesus. It means 'God saves'. That will be my prayer. That God saves him. That God saves me. That God saves Joseph. That God saves Elizabeth. And that I am given the strength to do what must be done, to cherish this child, to teach him, and walk with him safely through the world until that day when he will be made visible, and his light will scatter the darkness.

And now it is dark. This day is ended. The birdsong hushed. The flowers turned in on themselves. The mountains cool and silent. A new day awaits us.

I look out into the night. I remember the words of Isaiah and think that we have all been walking in darkness for far too long. But we didn't really know it; we got so used to it that it was strange and bewildering to encounter the light. But thrilling. Very thrilling. Full of grace and joy. That is what I carry: the light of the world, a light that shines in the darkness and the darkness cannot overcome it. I am the Lord's lantern. He has kindled a fire inside me.

Chapter 10

———•———

Isaiah

The people who walked in darkness have seen a great light; those who lived in a land of deep darkness—on them light has shined. You have multiplied the nation, you have increased its joy; they rejoice before you as with joy at the harvest, as people exult when dividing plunder. For the yoke of their burden, and the bar across their shoulders, the rod of their oppressor, you have broken as on the day of Midian. For all the boots of the tramping warriors and all the garments rolled in blood shall be burned as fuel for the fire. For a child has been born for us, a son given to us; authority rests upon his shoulders; and he is named Wonderful Counsellor, Mighty God, Everlasting Father, Prince of Peace. His authority shall grow continually, and there shall be endless peace.

Isaiah 9.2–7

This is what I say to the heavens, and this is what I say to the earth: these are the words that God has given me, making me his voice, and revealing to me the present as it is, and the future as it will be; the future as it will be with God, and the future as it will be if we go on forsaking God and turning from God's ways of peace. 'I reared children and brought them up,' says God, 'but they have rebelled against me. The ox knows its owner, and the donkey its master's crib; but Israel does not know me.

'What a sinful nation, people laden with iniquity, offspring who do evil, children who deal corruptly, why do you continue to rebel? The whole head is sick, and the whole heart faint. From the sole of the foot even to the head, there is no soundness in it, but bruises and sores and bleeding wounds; they have not been drained, or bound up, or softened with oil. Your country lies desolate, your cities are burned with fire; in your very presence aliens devour your land; it is desolate, as overthrown by foreigners. And the beloved daughter Zion is left like a booth in a vineyard, like a shelter in a cucumber field, like a besieged city.

'What to me is the multitude of your sacrifices?' says God. 'I have had enough of burnt-offerings of rams and the fat of fed beasts; I do not drink the blood of bulls or lambs or goats. When you come to appear before me, who asked this from your hand? Stop trampling my courts; bringing offerings is futile; incense is an abomination to me. I cannot endure your solemn assemblies. I hate your festivals. I am weary of them. Even though you make many prayers, when you stretch out your hands, I will hide my eyes from you; I will not listen; your hands are full of blood. Wash yourselves; make yourselves clean; remove the evil of your doings from before my eyes; cease to do evil, learn to do good; seek justice, rescue the oppressed, defend the orphan, plead for the widow.

'Come now, let us argue it out,' says God: 'though your sins are like scarlet, they shall be like snow; though they are red like crimson, they shall become like wool. If you are willing and obedient, you shall eat the good of the land; but if you refuse and rebel, you shall be devoured by the sword; for the mouth of God has spoken.'

And when I first heard these things, the words were like nails being driven into my head. That day in the Temple, when I first saw God's glory shining before me in terrible majesty and light, all I could see was my own unworthiness. You see, I have come to know about light and darkness. How sometimes they can be the same thing. For the greatest light of all, the light of the glorious majesty of God, if you see it, you will be blinded, plunged into darkness; and then you will see yourself as you really are.

Now I am called, with darkness approaching, and enemy forces converging, and the very forces of history and eternity conspiring, to speak about the light that is to come, and the fire that will purge.

For a seraphim flew from its attendance on God and anointed my mouth with a burning coal. My sins were forgiven, and I was made a messenger of God. For God spoke in the Temple that day, saying, 'Whom shall I send, and who will go for us?' And I replied, 'Here am I, send me.'

And having seen my own sins so clearly, I can also see the sins of the world, and how we call evil good and good evil, and darkness light and light darkness, and are wise in our own eyes. We have become valiant in drinking wine but acquit the guilty for a bribe, and deprive the innocent of their rights. But as the tongue of fire devours the stubble and as dry grass succumbs to the flame, so those who have turned their back on God's instructions and spurned his mercy will feel his anger kindled against them. Isn't it always the case with the fat and the rich? They add house to house and field to field, gathering more and more to themselves, building walls to protect themselves, but they end up alone. That is why God's light will become a fire and the fruitful land a desolation.

But even out of such a wretchedness a shoot shall remain, and out from the stock of Jesse a branch shall grow. That is what I see. That is what God will do. Yes, in the end, the boots of all the tramping warriors and all the garments rolled in blood shall be burned as fuel for the fire. A child will be born for us, a son given to us; authority will rest upon his shoulders, and he will be named Wonderful Counselor, Mighty God, Everlasting Father, Prince of Peace. His authority shall grow continually, and there shall be endless peace.

The spirit of God shall rest on him, the spirit of wisdom and understanding, the spirit of counsel and might, the spirit of knowledge and the fear of God. His delight shall be in the fear of God. He shall not judge by what his eyes see, or decide by what his ears hear; but with righteousness he shall judge the poor, and decide with equity for the meek of the earth; he shall strike the earth with the rod of his mouth, and with the breath of his lips he shall kill the wicked. Righteousness shall be the belt around his waist, and faithfulness the belt around his loins.

That is the day when God will say, 'Here is my servant, whom I uphold, my chosen, in whom my soul delights; I have put my spirit upon him; he will bring forth justice to the nations.

'He will not cry or lift up his voice, or make it heard in the street; a bruised reed he will not break, and a dimly burning wick he will not quench; he will faithfully bring forth justice. He will not grow faint or be crushed until he has established justice in the earth.'

And in that day, the day when he comes, and the day when we shall again return to the God who has returned to us, the wolf shall live with the lamb, the leopard shall lie down with the kid, the calf and the lion and the fatling together, and a little child shall lead them.

On that day the root of Jesse shall stand as a signal to the peoples; the nations shall inquire of him, and his dwelling shall be glorious.

And so, in the midst of all that is wretched, with calamity all about me, with my voice like the voice of a madman, naked, and soft of foot upon the hard earth, and with no one to listen, and with the coming certainty of utter hopelessness, darkness and despair about me, I sing out. I sing out with joy to the generous and mighty God who will shed his light upon the world; and I say back to the world, for this is the task God has given me, 'Arise, shine; for your light will come, and the glory of God will rise upon you.' For though darkness covers the earth, and thick darkness the people, the light of the glory of God will rise up, and God's glory will appear. Nations will come to this light, and kings—yes, the kings and rulers of the world—will come to the brightness of this new dawn. They shall bring gold and frankincense, and shall proclaim the praises of God. Where forests were destroyed, the glory of Lebanon shall come—the cypress, the plane and the pine—to beautify the place of God's dwelling. God's peace will oversee the world: the Prince of Peace, the one whose coming will be light and joy. And violence shall be no more, nor devastation or destruction.

The sun shall no longer be the light by day, nor for brightness shall the moon give light by night; but God, and the one whom God sends: the one I see but cannot see, the one who will bear our infirmities and carry our diseases, and be wounded for our transgressions and crushed for our iniquities, and by whose wounds we will be healed. And God will be our glory. The sun shall no more go down, nor the moon withdraw itself; for God will be the everlasting light. All the days of mourning in the world shall be ended.

What does all this mean? I see it and can't see it. I know it, but can't know it. It comes to me like the sweetest music imaginable, and at the same time gall and bitterness. I see the horrors we do to each other and the iniquity we revel in, and the bile we pour out upon the world. I see the injustices, the calamities and the pain. I see it as gathering, glowering darkness; and at the same time I see this great light coming. I see it in the fragility of the sign that God gave me to give to those who kept on demanding a sign: a young woman is with child and she will bear a son and name him Emmanuel, a name that means 'God is with us'. Somehow, somewhere, God is going to do this. God is going to do it in a way that is manageable, in a way that we can see it and not be blinded, in a way that may even mean we can reflect such glory and live in peace. A young woman will bear a son, and that child will be the light of the world, and those who follow will never be in darkness, but will have the light of life.

And I see all sorts of other things that I do not readily understand, but I faithfully tell them without really knowing what I'm telling, except that it is from God. But if we choose not to follow—if the pot turns on the potter, and says, 'I don't need you any longer', if the thing that is created says to its maker, 'You did not make me, you have no understanding and nothing to teach me or give me', if things are turned this upside-down, and if we determine to keep our deeds in the dark thinking no one sees or knows—then there is indeed a night of terrible obscurity descended on the world. We will make it our home, and glower with rage at any who come near, even the one who is himself the light. We will turn our backs on him, and scrabbling for scraps in the blackness of our own shadow (for his light will still be there) we will have chosen darkness.

This child, who will have authority resting upon him and will bear peace, will, therefore, also be a servant who suffers and who bears the sins of many. He will enter into the depths of that darkness to show us what it means to live the right way up. And only by sharing in its depths and its dreads can peace and light radiate into the farthest corners of our retreat into ourselves and the darkness we prefer. And now I see something else (something terrible and yet so beautiful that words are going to slip and fail): coming from Bozrah, his garments stained crimson, splendidly robed and in great might, and announcing vindication and victory, and coming to save. And I cry out: 'Why are your robes red, and your garments like theirs who tread the wine press?' He replies: 'I have trodden the wine press alone, and from the peoples no one was with me. For the day of vengeance was in my heart, and the year for my redeeming work had come.'

So, though I cannot understand it, I see it and believe it and rejoice in it, trapped and burdened as I am by the darkness of this passing age. I recount what God will do; and for my succor remember what God has done: his mighty deeds from of old, the great favor he has shown to the house of Israel because of his mercy and according to the abundance of his steadfast love. For in the past God himself became their savior in their day of distress. It wasn't a messenger or even an angel that saved them, but his presence. In his love and pity, God redeemed them himself; he visited his people, he lifted them up and carried them all the days of old.

But just as they rebelled then, they rebel now; and will, no doubt, go on rebelling and grieving God's Holy Spirit. And won't it always be like this? Won't the human heart always rebel? Won't our eyes always turn away? Therefore God has become our enemy; not that this was what God wanted, or chose: it is because we prefer darkness to light and are too easily blinded by the light of God and beguiled by the lights of the world.

But there have been times when we have remembered the past, and what God did in it. We have remembered Moses,

God's servant, a man who met with God face-to-face and saw things clearly. It was through Moses that God brought his people up out of the sea, and divided the waters before them to make for himself an everlasting name: Wonderful Counselor, Mighty God, Everlasting Father, Prince of Peace.

Will God do this again? Will he speak to us face-to-face?

Chapter 11

———•———

Moses

Moses was keeping the flock of his father-in-law Jethro, the priest of Midian; he led his flock beyond the wilderness, and came to Horeb, the mountain of God. There the angel of the LORD appeared to him in a flame of fire out of a bush; he looked, and the bush was blazing, yet it was not consumed. Then Moses said, 'I must turn aside and look at this great sight, and see why the bush is not burned up.' When the LORD saw that he had turned aside to see, God called to him out of the bush, 'Moses, Moses!' And he said, 'Here I am.' Then he said, 'Come no closer! Remove the sandals from your feet, for the place on which you are standing is holy ground.' He said further, 'I am the God of your father, the God of Abraham, the God of Isaac, and the God of Jacob.' And Moses hid his face, for he was afraid to look at God. Then the LORD said, 'I have observed the misery of my people who are in Egypt; I have heard their cry on account of their taskmasters. Indeed, I know their sufferings, and I have come down to deliver them from the Egyptians, and to bring them up out of that land to a good and broad land, a land flowing with milk and honey.'

Exodus 3.1–8

The wind whistles and rattles across the plain. Harsh and unforgiving, it scours the land, and few things grow. You hear it, and you don't hear it. It is here, and it is gone. There is a dread chill in the air. Eventually it gets inside you. Then one day the cold earth claims you for its own, and holds you fast till you become part of the earth, fused with the rocks and dispersed in the sand.

The little scrubby scraps of vegetation that can survive this climate cling to the same rocks for life. They blossom and flower. They fade. The wind blows over them. They are gone.

It is nearly evening. It goes on. The cycle of the days. The rhythm of the seasons. All the little lives that populate the world. Somewhere a birth. Somewhere else a death. A couple, hiding in the shadows, unite their bodies in a brief ecstasy. And afterwards hold each other tight, knowing that love can conquer. Don't despise it. Each act of love is a small defiance against the dying light. But somewhere else, there will be a random cruelty. Or a child begging for bread.

The dice are loaded. The day finished, its color sucked into the empty palate of the night. There is no sunset to charm us. The clouds that have hung low all day obscure the sun.

Balanced in the scales we count for nothing. Squalor and misery and fear weigh heavy on our hearts. We brood upon the future; and each night is a daily reminder of looming death. The whole world is descending into inky blackness. What life there is has retreated, burrowing into safety beneath the ground. Soon we will do the same. Soon the creatures of the night will hunt and prowl.

But what of me? What have I achieved? Where am I going?

I have been privileged beyond imagining; brought up by Pharaoh himself, but always an outsider. And now an outcast as well.

I am frightened by the anger inside me. I do things that I don't want to do. The things I do want to do, I neglect. There is no health in me: only, for so much of the time, a steady, simmering rage. Where has it come from? Where will it lead?

I hated the way the Egyptians treated my people. No one deserves to live like that, to be made a slave and yoked to another's control. It was wrong to let my anger boil over, but when I saw one of my countrymen being beaten and humiliated, I could not stop myself. I killed the man quickly and efficiently.

It was surprising how easy it was. His neck snapped like the branch of a young sapling; and before my eyes, and without any actual blood on my hands, his body fell limp to the ground. Once he had life. Then he didn't. Life was suddenly very fragile and very cheap. Mine, to dispose of as I chose.

I hated myself for that. I hid his body in the sand and ran off. I thought that no one had seen me. But the next day, when I tried to break up a stupid fight between two fellow Hebrews, one of them turned on me, saying, 'Who made you a ruler and judge over us? Are you going to kill me as well?' Then I was afraid. If it is known, then soon Pharaoh will know, and his favor towards me will quickly vanish.

So I fled. I came here to the land of Midian, and because I helped him, Reuel offered me food and rest. I married his daughter Zipporah. They have been good to me. I have here a life—of sorts. And a son, Gershom. But I am still a stranger here. I am still an alien. And my people still groan under the bondage of Pharaoh. They cry out to God, but God doesn't seem to hear them. And God doesn't seem to hear me. I know I have failed. But I don't know how to start again. I know I have led a half-life—half accepted, cushioned by Pharaoh's favor; and half rejected, a Hebrew underneath. I am an Egyptian, but not an Egyptian. I am a Hebrew, but not a Hebrew. That is me. I don't fit. So I lashed out in both directions. And I have retreated to this wilderness; this dread half-place, where half-wits and half-castes don't sully the view.

But today it changed. That is why I am drawing a line in the sand. Today, what goes around now goes forward. I still carry the fears and doubts and miseries that make a lifetime. But I am carrying them somewhere. And it is why I am still sitting here in the half-light, half-dark of today's ending.

I have let the fire go cold. The last few embers throb, inter-mittent and faint, like the fading pulse of a dying man. But I don't need the fire anymore. I have seen something else today. Also a fire: incandescent and vast like the sky in the morn-ing on a clear day when the sun rises, only contained and luminously bright, in this one place rather than everywhere. And by this light I have seen another course through the wil-derness and it has changed me; and eventually, in what lies ahead at the end of many journeys—or will it be just one?—a greater light will dawn upon the world.

Now I hear the first sounds of the nighttime. I shiver in its chill and unforgiving grasp. An owl hoots. Further afield a mountain cat pounces upon its kill, and the poor creature whose neck is held in that same vice-like grip of death of which I know my own hands are capable cries out.

At first it seemed an apparition—a mirage, like the illusion of water, shimmering on the near horizon of a flat plain on a dry day when the sun is high. But there was no sun today. Only clouds and a gathering gloom. Perhaps it was the sound of its crackle and spit that stopped me, and fixed me. Or was it the heat? Or the stench of sulphur on the air? Now all my ques-tions, my excuses, and even my doubts about myself, have been purged and refined. Who am I, that I should do this thing for God? And why doesn't God send somebody else? And I've never been very good with words. There are others better qualified than me. There are people with wisdom and faith and self-control. They are the ones that God should call. They are the ones that God should send.

All these were gone. Answered. I saw ahead of me a burning bush, ablaze with a thrilling intensity, but not consumed. It drew me. It confounded and amazed me. For all too well do I know fiery passions that consume. They ignite inside me, and they have almost devoured me. But this was passion of equal intensity: raging, rousing, its flames licking the sky, its sparks dazzling; but the bush was not burned up. It was illuminated. And so was I. Turning aside to that bright illumination, drawn like the face of a flower to the sun, like iron filings to a magnet, like a lover to her beloved, I heard a voice calling me: 'Moses, Moses.' And I said, gently, confidently, 'Here I am.' And the voice said, 'Come no closer! Remove the sandals from your feet, for the place on which you are standing is holy ground.'

So I stood there, barefoot before the fire, amazed and heartened by a power that irradiated but did not destroy, and I felt like one reborn. All in a moment, in a twinkling, in a conflagration, I was changed. I know it sounds stupid. Can a man enter his mother's womb and be born again? Well, perhaps. That is how it felt today. For it was God's voice speaking to me out of the burning bush. I know it now. I knew it then. Instantly and irrevocably. I turned my face away as the voice said, 'I am the God of your father, the God of Abraham, the God of Isaac, and the God of Jacob. I have heard the cry of my people. I know their sufferings. I have come to deliver them.'

Then, when all my excuses for not being part of God's purposes were exhausted, I said, as much in desperation as in hope (there is, after all, always a conflict within me): 'If the people you are asking me to deliver from bondage say to me, who is it that sent you, and what is his name, how shall I reply?'

God then said to me, 'I AM WHO I AM. Say to the people, I AM has sent me.'

Now the darkness thickens. The razor of the wind sharpens. The cold drills into my bones. Night arrives.

'I AM has sent me.'

I peer down the tunnel of my own future: the sunsets and tomorrows of a lifetime, and beyond it to a good land, a land where milk and honey flow, even the consoling breasts of a mother whose motherhood was denied and threatened; and beyond it to many other lifetimes, and the many treacheries and failings that will beset this people I am called to save; until there is another, born out of the blazing fire of another revelation, from the depths of someone ordinary like me who is also able to say yes to God; suckled at the breast of such a faithful one, his presence will scatter the darkness, and his light will burn forever. He is also called 'I AM'. And he is the same. He will not allow his people to be slaves. He will search out the lost. He will care for the lowly. He will turn every stone. His voice will be in the faltering tongue of a nation yet to be born, but as numerous as the stars in the sky or the grains of sand upon the shore. He will be brilliant light. He will be salvation. He will be born into the darkness of an unknowing world. He will go down into the night.

Annunciation: a poem

There is only one thing that prevents
The gentle movement, heaven into earth:
Not the fear which godly greeting brings,
Nor cold presumption (God could never speak),
Nor empty tomb, nor barren heart,
Nor eyes searching, voices how long blaze,
Nor the silence where there should be praise,
Nor the bitter taste of human failing;
But the lack of trust that what was promised
Might in human flesh be born, achieved,
How happy she who for us all believed,
Strength of God in human weakness blending,
Tenderly the humble servant lifted,
From the fetal cry the fatal mending.

A prayer

. . . wise men at the end know dark is right.

Dylan Thomas, 1914–53

Bring us, O Lord, at our last awakening
into that house and gate of heaven,
to enter into that gate and dwell in that house
where shall be no darkness or dazzling, but one equal light;
no noise nor silence, but one equal music;
no fears nor hopes, but one equal possession;
no ends nor beginnings, but one equal eternity
in the habitations of your glory and dominion,
world without end.

John Donne, 1572–1631

CPSIA information can be obtained at www.ICGtesting.com
Printed in the USA
LVOW07s1210181115

463039LV00007B/18/P